DATE DUE

JAN 0 2 2013			

DISCARD

CT 1 3 2008

Demco, Inc. 38-293

BROADBAND INTERNET: ACCESS, REGULATION AND POLICY

BROADBAND INTERNET: ACCESS, REGULATION AND POLICY

ELLEN S. COHEN
EDITOR

Nova Science Publishers, Inc.
New York

For permission to use material from this book please contact us:
Telephone 631-231-7269; Fax 631-231-8175
Web Site: http://www.novapublishers.com

NOTICE TO THE READER

The Publisher has taken reasonable care in the preparation of this book, but makes no expressed or implied warranty of any kind and assumes no responsibility for any errors or omissions. No liability is assumed for incidental or consequential damages in connection with or arising out of information contained in this book. The Publisher shall not be liable for any special, consequential, or exemplary damages resulting, in whole or in part, from the readers' use of, or reliance upon, this material.

Independent verification should be sought for any data, advice or recommendations contained in this book. In addition, no responsibility is assumed by the publisher for any injury and/or damage to persons or property arising from any methods, products, instructions, ideas or otherwise contained in this publication.

This publication is designed to provide accurate and authoritative information with regard to the subject matter covered herein. It is sold with the clear understanding that the Publisher is not engaged in rendering legal or any other professional services. If legal or any other expert assistance is required, the services of a competent person should be sought. FROM A DECLARATION OF PARTICIPANTS JOINTLY ADOPTED BY A COMMITTEE OF THE AMERICAN BAR ASSOCIATION AND A COMMITTEE OF PUBLISHERS.

LIBRARY OF CONGRESS CATALOGING-IN-PUBLICATION DATA

Broadband Internet : acess, regulation, and policy / Ellen S. Cohen, editor.
       p. cm.
   ISBN: 978-1-60456-073-2 (hardcover)
   1. Broadband communication systems. 2. Internet. 3. Digital subscriber lines. I. Cohen, Ellen S.
TK5103.4.B7644 2008
384--dc22
                         2007040361

Published by Nova Science Publishers, Inc. ✦ *New York*

CONTENTS

PREFACE

The internet has become so widespread that such issues as access, regulation and related policies have become major factors in the economy and social fabric of societies in every part of the world. Peoples without running water are demanding access to the internet and those without it are becoming deprived citizens. This new book examines current issues of interest to the blossoming area.

Chapter 1 - Debate has begun about what statutory and regulatory framework is most likely to foster innovation and investment both in physical broadband networks *and* in the applications that ride over those networks. Perhaps the most contentious element in that debate is whether competitive marketplace forces are sufficient to constrain the broadband network providers from restricting independent applications providers' access to their networks in a fashion that would harm consumers and innovation.

The telephone and cable companies are deploying wireline broadband networks with unique architectures. For example, Verizon is deploying optical fiber all the way to the customer premise, while AT and T is deploying fiber to a node and then using DSL over existing copper lines to reach the customer premise, and Comcast and other cable companies are deploying a hybrid fiber-coaxial cable network. But in each case, their broadband networks have the same basic structure, with three primary components — the broadband "last mile" grid to end-user customers, the company's proprietary IP network, and the company's facilities in what has traditionally been called the internet backbone (and is often referred to as the "public internet"). This report analyzes these three components to identify the parameters that network providers have within their control (such as their choices about network architecture, overall bandwidth capacity, bandwidth reserved for their own use, traffic prioritization, the terms and rates for access to their networks and for their retail services) that can affect how end users and independent applications providers can access their networks, how those parameters contribute to the management and operation of the network, and how those parameters might be used strategically to harm competition for, and consumers of, voice over internet protocol (VoIP), video, and other applications that ride over broadband networks.

The report then reviews various legislative proposals affecting network access to assess their potential impact on broadband network providers' ability to manage their networks and to practice anticompetitive strategic behavior. Two bills, H.R. 5252 as passed by the House and H.R. 5252 as amended by the Senate Commerce Committee (originally introduced as S. 2686), specify particular consumer rights to broadband access. Three bills — H.R. 5273, S.

2360, and S. 2917 — propose variations on "network neutrality" rules that have provisions affecting the access of independent applications providers, as well as consumers, to broadband networks. Two other bills, H.R. 5417 and S. 2113, propose modification of existing competition law (involving antitrust and unfair methods of competition) to explicitly address broadband access issues. This report will be updated as warranted.

Chapter 2 - Technological advances and deregulatory actions now allow consumers to obtain their local and long distance telephone services, their high-speed Internet services, and their video services from competing technologies . The convergence of previously distinct markets has required companies to seek strategies for holding on to their traditional customers while seeking new ones . One of those strategies is for companies to offer bundles of "traditional" and "new" services at a single price that often represents a discount off the sum of the prices of the individual services . These bundled service offerings are favored by many consumers . They provide the convenience of "one stop shopping" and in some situations, by providing the full panoply of services at a fixed price, make it easier for consumers to comparison shop . They also are favored by many providers because they tend to reduce "churn" - the rate at which customers shift to competitors - and allow providers to exploit economies of scope in marketing .

But bundling also can create public policy issues for Congress . The bundled offerings typically provide some combination of interstate telecommunications services, intrastate telecommunications services, and non-telecommunications services (information services, video services, and even customer premises equipment) for a single price . The federal Universal Service Fund - the federal subsidy program that assures affordable telephone rates for high-cost (rural) and low-income telephone customers as well as for schools, libraries, and rural health facilities - is supported by an assessment on interstate telecommunications revenues only. But it is difficult to identify the portion of revenues generated by a bundled service offering attributable to the interstate telecommunications portion of that bundle. There is no unambiguous way for providers to assign a portion of the bundled price to interstate telecommunications services or for fund administrators to audit that assignment. In addition, some taxes are assessed upon one or more, but not all, of the services included in various bundled service offerings . This creates the same assessment and auditing problem for these taxes as exists for the federal Universal Service Fund. This has important policy implications at a time when many Members of Congress seek to shelter Internet services-which often are included in these bundles- from taxation without placing any group of providers at a competitive advantage or disadvantage .

Some observers have been concerned that bundled service offerings could have anticompetitive consequences if they foster industry consolidation or if a provider has market power for one of the services in its bundled offering and can use that offering to tie that service to a competitive service in a fashion that reduces competition for the competitive service .

Leaders in both the House and the Senate Commerce Committees have announced that in the 109" Congress they plan to review and reform the 1996 Telecommunications Act (P.L .104-104) in light of the market convergence that underlies the trend toward bundling . This report will be updated as events warrant.

Chapter 3 - Ormation haves and have-nots," or in other words, between those Americans who use or have access to telecommunications technologies (e.g., telephones, computers, the Internet) and those who do not. One important subset of the digital divide debate concerns high-speed Internet access, also known as *broadband*. Broadband is provided by a series of technologies (e.g. cable, telephone wire, fiber, satellite, wireless) that give users the ability to send and receive data at volumes and speeds far greater than current "dial-up" Internet access over traditional telephone lines.

Broadband technologies are currently being deployed primarily by the private sector throughout the United States. While the numbers of new broadband subscribers continue to grow, studies conducted by the Federal Communications Commission (FCC), the Department of Commerce (DOC), and the Department of Agriculture (USDA) suggest that the rate of broadband deployment in urban and high income areas may be outpacing deployment in rural and low-income areas.

Some policymakers, believing that disparities in broadband access across American society could have adverse economic and social consequences on those left behind, assert that the federal government should play a more active role to avoid a "digital divide" in broadband access. One approach is for the federal government to provide financial assistance to support broadband deployment in underserved areas. Others, however, believe that federal assistance for broadband deployment is not appropriate. Some opponents question the reality of the "digital divide," and argue that federal intervention in the broadband marketplace would be premature and, in some cases, counterproductive.

Legislation introduced (but not enacted) in the 109th Congress sought to provide federal financial assistance for broadband deployment in the form of grants, loans, subsidies, and tax credits. Many of these legislative proposals are likely to be reintroduced into the 110th Congress. Of particular note is the possible reauthorization of the Rural Utilities Service (RUS) broadband program, which is expected to be considered as part of the 2007 farm bill. Legislation to reform universal service – which could have a significant impact on the amount of financial assistance available for broadband deployment in rural and underserved areas – has been introduced into the 110th Congress (H.R. 42, S. 101).

In assessing such legislation, several policy issues arise. For example, is the current status of broadband deployment data an adequate basis on which to base policy decisions? Is federal assistance premature, or do the risks of delaying assistance to underserved areas outweigh the benefits of avoiding federal intervention in the marketplace? And finally, if one assumes that governmental action is necessary to spur broadband deployment in underserved areas, which specific approaches, either separately or in combination, are likely to be most effective?

Chapter 4 - Broadband or high-speed Internet access is provided by a series of technologies that give users the ability to send and receive data at volumes and speeds far greater than current Internet access over traditional telephone lines. In addition to offering speed, broadband access provides a continuous, "always on" connection and the ability to both receive (download) and transmit (upload) data at high speeds. Broadband access, along with the content and services it might enable, has the potential to transform the Internet: both what it offers and how it is used. It is likely that many of the future applications that will best exploit the technological capabilities of broadband have yet to be developed. There are multiple transmission media or technologies that can be used to provide broadband access. These include cable, an enhanced telephone service called digital subscriber line (DSL), satellite, fixed wireless (including "wi-fi" and "Wi-Max"), broadband over powerline (BPL), fiber-to-the-home (FTTH), and others. While many (though not all) offices and businesses now have Internet broadband access, a remaining challenge is providing broadband over "the last mile" to consumers in their homes. Currently, a number of competing telecommunications companies are developing, deploying, and marketing specific technologies and services that provide residential broadband access.

From a public policy perspective, the goals are to ensure that broadband deployment is timely and contributes to the nation's economic growth, that industry competes fairly, and that service is provided to all sectors and geographical locations of American society. The federal government — through Congress and the Federal Communications Commission (FCC) — is seeking to ensure fair competition among the players so that broadband will be available and affordable in a timely manner to all Americans who want it.

While President Bush has set a goal of universal broadband availability by 2007, some areas of the nation — particularly rural and low-income communities —continue to lack full access to high-speed broadband Internet service. In order to address this problem, the 109th Congress is examining the scope and effect of federal broadband financial assistance programs (including universal service), and the impact of telecommunications regulation and new technologies on broadband deployment. One facet of the debate over broadband services focuses on whether present laws and subsequent regulatory policies are needed to ensure the development of competition and its subsequent consumer benefits, or conversely, whether such laws and regulations are overly burdensome and discourage needed investment in and deployment of broadband services. The Congressional debate has focused on H.R. 5252 which addresses a number of issues, including the extent to which legacy regulations should be applied to traditional providers as they enter new markets, the extent to which legacy regulations should be imposed on new entrants as they compete with traditional providers in their markets, the treatment of new and converging technologies, and the emergence of municipal broadband networks and Internet access. This report — which will be updated as events warrant — replaces CRS Issue Brief IB10045, *Broadband Internet Regulation and Access: Background and Issues*.

Chapter 5 - Given the large potential impact broadband access to the Internet may have on the economic development of rural America, concern has been raised over a "digital divide" between rural and urban or suburban areas with respect to broadband deployment. While there are many examples of rural communities with state of the art telecommunications facilities, recent surveys and studies have indicated that, in general, rural areas tend to lag behind urban and suburban areas in broadband deployment.

Citing the lagging deployment of broadband in many rural areas, Congress and the Administration acted in 2001 and 2002 to initiate pilot broadband loan and grant programs within the Rural Utilities Service (RUS) at the U.S. Department of Agriculture (USDA). Subsequently, Section 6103 of the Farm Security and Rural Investment Act of 2002 (P.L. 107-171) amended the Rural Electrification Act of 1936 to authorize a loan and loan guarantee program to provide funds for the costs of the construction, improvement, and acquisition of facilities and equipment for broadband service in eligible rural communities. Currently, RUS/USDA houses the only two federal assistance programs *exclusively* dedicated to financing broadband deployment: the Rural Broadband Access Loan and Loan Guarantee Program and the Community Connect Grant Program.

RUS broadband loan and grant programs have been awarding funds to entities serving rural communities since FY2001. A number of criticisms of the RUS broadband loan and grant programs have emerged, including criticisms related to loan approval and the application process, eligibility criteria, and loans to communities with existing providers.

The current authorization for the Rural Broadband Access Loan and Loan Guarantee Program expires on September 30, 2007. It is expected that the 110th Congress will consider reauthorization of the program as part of the farm bill. Some key issues pertinent to a consideration of the RUS broadband programs include restrictions on applicant eligibility, how "rural" is defined with respect to eligible rural communities, how to address assistance to areas with pre-existing broadband service, technological neutrality, funding levels and mechanisms, and the appropriateness of federal assistance. Ultimately, any modification of rules, regulations, or criteria associated with the RUS broadband program will likely result in "winners and losers" in terms of which companies, communities, regions of the country, and technologies are eligible or more likely to receive broadband loans and grants.

This report will be updated as events warrant.

Chapter 6 - Congress has expressed significant interest in increasing the availability of broadband services throughout the nation, both in expanding the geographic availability of such services, as well as expanding the service choices available to consumers. Broadband over Powerlines (BPL) has the potential to play a significant role in increasing the competitive landscape of the communications industry but also has the potential to extend the reach of broadband to a greater number of Americans. BPL, like any technology, has its advantages and disadvantages. Proponents state that (1) BPL is less expensive to deploy than the cable and telephone companies' broadband offerings, (2) it does not require upgrades to the actual electric grid, and (3) it is not limited by certain technical constraints of its competitors. However, critics have expressed ongoing concern that BPL could interfere with licensed radio spectrum such as amateur radio, government, and emergency response frequencies.

The Federal Communications Commission (FCC) began investigating BPL in 2003 and adopted a Report and Order (FCC 04-245) in its proceeding in October 2004. Among other items, the Order

- set forth rules imposing new technical requirements on BPL devices;
- established bands within which BPL must avoid operating entirely and "exclusion zones" within which BPL must avoid operating on certain frequencies;
- established a publicly available BPL notification database to facilitate resolution of harmful interference; and
- improved measurement procedures for all equipment that use RF energy to communicate over power lines.

Other FCC proceedings are also related to BPL development, deployment, and regulation. For instance, the Commission ruled on August 5, 2005, that providers of certain voice over Internet Protocol (VoIP) services — such as BPL providers —would be required to accommodate law enforcement wiretaps.

On April 21, 2005, Representative Mike Ross introduced H.Res. 230, to express the sense that the FCC should reconsider and revise its rules governing BPL. The resolution was referred to the Committee on Energy and Commerce Subcommittee on Telecommunications and the Internet on May 13, 2005. Additionally, on April 26, 2006, Mr. Ross introduced an amendment (#25) in committee to the Communications Opportunity, Promotion, and Enhancement Act of 2006 (H.R. 5252) that would require the FCC to study and report on the interference potential of BPL systems within 90 days of the bill's enactment. The amendment passed on a voice vote.

On August 3, 2006, the FCC adopted a Memorandum Opinion and Order acknowledging the significant benefits of BPL, reaffirming its commitment to address interference issues, and reemphasizing that the Part 15 rule changes were made to ensure that BPL operations do not become a source of interference to licensed radio services.

Chapter 7 - In 2002, the Federal Communications Commission (FCC) issued a *Declaratory Ruling and Notice of Proposed Rulemaking* regarding the provision of Internet services over cable connections to address the legal status of such services under the Communications Act of 1934, as amended. In the *Declaratory Ruling*, the Commission determined that "cable modem service, as it is currently offered, is properly classified as an interstate information service, not as a cable service, and that there is no separate offering of telecommunications service." By classifying cable modem service as an information service and not a telecommunications service or a hybrid information and telecommunications service, the Commission precluded the mandatory application of the requirements imposed on common carriers under Title II of the Communications Act, thus allowing the provision of such services to develop with relatively few regulatory requirements.

There were numerous challenges to the FCC's classification of cable modem service as an information service, which were consolidated, and by judicial lottery assigned to the Ninth Circuit for review. The Ninth Circuit, applying its own interpretation of the act, vacated the FCC's ruling regarding the classification of cable modem service as an information service. On appeal, the Supreme Court overturned the Ninth Circuit's decision, finding that the FCC's interpretation of the act was "reasonable" in light of the statute's ambiguity. The Court's decision revives the FCC's classification of cable modem service as an "information service" and refocuses attention on several important issues regarding the regulation of broadband services that Congress is likely to consider in its reexamination of the Telecommunications Act of 1996.

This chapter provides an overview of the regulatory actions leading up to and an analysis of the Supreme Court's decision in *National Cable and Telecommunications Association v. Brand X Internet Services*. It also provides a discussion of the possible legal and economic implications of the Court's decision. The report will be updated as events warrant.

In: Broadband Internet: Access, Regulation and Policy   ISBN: 978-1-60456-073-2
Editor: Ellen S. Cohen, pp. 1-26   © 2007 Nova Science Publishers, Inc.

Chapter 1

ACCESS TO BROADBAND NETWORKS*

Charles B. Goldfarb

Industrial Organization and Telecommunications Policy Resources,
Science, and Industry Division

ABSTRACT

Debate has begun about what statutory and regulatory framework is most likely to foster innovation and investment both in physical broadband networks *and* in the applications that ride over those networks. Perhaps the most contentious element in that debate is whether competitive marketplace forces are sufficient to constrain the broadband network providers from restricting independent applications providers' access to their networks in a fashion that would harm consumers and innovation.

The telephone and cable companies are deploying wireline broadband networks with unique architectures. For example, Verizon is deploying optical fiber all the way to the customer premise, while AT and T is deploying fiber to a node and then using DSL over existing copper lines to reach the customer premise, and Comcast and other cable companies are deploying a hybrid fiber-coaxial cable network. But in each case, their broadband networks have the same basic structure, with three primary components — the broadband "last mile" grid to end-user customers, the company's proprietary IP network, and the company's facilities in what has traditionally been called the internet backbone (and is often referred to as the "public internet"). This report analyzes these three components to identify the parameters that network providers have within their control (such as their choices about network architecture, overall bandwidth capacity, bandwidth reserved for their own use, traffic prioritization, the terms and rates for access to their networks and for their retail services) that can affect how end users and independent applications providers can access their networks, how those parameters contribute to the management and operation of the network, and how those parameters might be used strategically to harm competition for, and consumers of, voice over internet protocol (VoIP), video, and other applications that ride over broadband networks.

The report then reviews various legislative proposals affecting network access to assess their potential impact on broadband network providers' ability to manage their networks and to practice anticompetitive strategic behavior. Two bills, H.R. 5252 as

---

* Excerpted from CRS Report RL33496, dated August 31, 2006.

passed by the House and H.R. 5252 as amended by the Senate Commerce Committee (originally introduced as S. 2686), specify particular consumer rights to broadband access. Three bills — H.R. 5273, S. 2360, and S. 2917 — propose variations on "network neutrality" rules that have provisions affecting the access of independent applications providers, as well as consumers, to broadband networks. Two other bills, H.R. 5417 and S. 2113, propose modification of existing competition law (involving antitrust and unfair methods of competition) to explicitly address broadband access issues. This report will be updated as warranted.

INTRODUCTION

Debate has begun about what statutory and regulatory framework is most likely to foster innovation and investment both in physical broadband networks *and* in the applications that ride over those networks. Perhaps the most contentious element in that debate is whether competitive marketplace forces are sufficient to constrain the broadband network providers from restricting independent applications providers' access to their networks in a fashion that would harm consumers and innovation. Or is government intervention needed in the form of what has been referred to as "network neutrality," unfair competitive practices, or other nondiscrimination rules placed on the network providers?

This debate has been stimulated by some fundamental changes in the telecommunications market environment — several technology-driven, several market-driven, and one regulatory-driven.

- Digital technology has reduced the costs for those firms that already have single-use (for example, voice or video) networks to upgrade their networks in order to offer multiple services over their single platform. The cost for these previously single-service providers to enter new service markets has been significantly reduced,[1] inducing market convergence. Most notably, cable companies are upgrading their networks to offer voice and data services as well as video services, and telephone companies are upgrading their networks to offer video and data services as well as voice services.

- Despite these lower entry costs, however, wireline broadband networks require huge sunk up-front fixed capital expenditures. This may limit the number of efficient broadband networks that can be deployed in any market to two (the cable provider and the wireline telephone company) unless a lower cost alternative becomes available using wireless or some other new technology.[2]

- Although wireless technology may provide a third or even fourth alternative, it is not likely to be a ubiquitous option anytime soon.[3] The commercial mobile wireless (cellphone), WiFi, and WiMAX technologies still require significant further technical developments before they will be able to provide comparable service and operate at the necessary scale. Moreover, spectrum is just being made available for these technologies, and in many cases parties currently using that spectrum must be moved to other spectrum.

- The new broadband networks are able to deliver potentially highly valued services, such as voice over internet protocol (VoIP) and video over internet protocol (IP

Video), that are qualitatively different than most of the services that have been provided over the internet in the past. Where services such as e-mail and website searches are not sensitive to "latency" — the amount of time it takes a packet of data to travel from source to destination — these new services are sensitive to delays in the delivery of packets of bits due to congestion or other problems.[4] As a result, the traditional internet "best effort" standard that does not guarantee that delays will not occur may be insufficient to meet customers' service quality requirements for these new latency-sensitive services.[5] More intensive network management may be needed to meet these quality of service (packet delivery) requirements.

- Equipment is being deployed in the broadband networks that can identify both the source of individual packets and the application to which individual packets are being put. With this equipment, network providers can give some packets higher priority than others, which can ensure that specific quality of service requirements are being met, but also could be abused to discriminate for or against particular applications or applications providers.
- Some new applications place very substantial bandwidth demands on the public internet and proprietary IP networks. For example, one industry analyst estimated that one particular application, BitTorrent software that uses file-sharing technology to download movies and other content, accounted for as much as 30% of all internet traffic at the end of 2004, and that peer-to-peer (P2P) applications, in general, represented 60% of internet traffic.[6] BitTorrent has been used both for legitimate purposes and for the illegal downloading of copyrighted materials, but has now been accepted by some mainstream content providers. For example, Warner Brothers has announced plans to make hundreds of movies and television shows available for purchase over the internet using BitTorrent software.[7] Other major industry players, such as Microsoft and Sony, have introduced movie download services that use P2P technology.
- Although the telephone and cable companies are deploying different network architectures,[8] they are pursuing business plans and regulatory strategies with the same key elements:
- They expect latency-sensitive video and voice services to be the "killer applications" that will generate the revenues needed to justify upgrade and buildout of their physical broadband networks.
- To minimize customer churn[9] and to gain an advantage over providers of single services, they market bundles of voice, data, and video services, with discounts that are greater the greater the number of services purchased. (It is expected by many that this "triple-play" bundle will be expanded to a "quadruple-play" bundle with the addition of mobile wireless service.)
- The set of services the telephone and cable companies plan to offer over their networks, despite having interactive components, follow the model of the customer being primarily a recipient of information, not a transmitter of information. Therefore the broadband network architecture they all are deploying is asymmetric — with significantly greater bandwidth available from the broadband provider to the customer than in the reverse direction.
- The video and voice services they offer, as well as other end-to-end services they plan to offer in the future, require quality of service assurances that they claim are

not available on the "public internet," but can be provided on their proprietary IP networks. In order to assure the quality of service of their own offerings, the broadband network providers all seek to manage bandwidth usage on their proprietary broadband networks by reserving a significant proportion of their network capacity for their own applications and by controlling the access that independent applications providers have to those networks through a variety of means, including charges for priority access.

- The Federal Communications Commission ("FCC" or "Commission") ruled in 2002 that cable modem service offered by cable companies, despite having a telecommunications component, is an information service and therefore not subject to the common carrier regulations imposed on telecommunications services in Title II of the Communications Act.[10] The FCC decision was upheld by the Supreme Court in June 2005.[11] Subsequently, the FCC ruled that DSL service offered by cable companies also is an information service.[12] As a result, neither cable modem service nor DSL service is subject to the interconnection, nondiscrimination, and access requirements of Title II.

Independent applications providers have voiced concern that the broadband network providers could abuse that control over network access to constrain — or entirely exclude — them from competing in the provision of applications, thereby undermining their ability to bring innovative applications to consumers. Some applications providers therefore have proposed enactment of statutory and regulatory requirements, such as nondiscriminatory access to broadband networks or network neutrality requirements. Others have been less confident about the ability to craft effective nondiscrimination or neutrality rules. They have suggested that government policy that promotes entry by broadband network providers that do not share the business plans of the cable and telephone companies might be a more effective way to foster innovation and investment in applications.[13] This might include prohibiting restrictions on municipal deployment of broadband networks, expediting the availability of spectrum for wireless broadband networks, and limiting the amount of such spectrum that can be acquired by companies owned by or in other ways affiliated with the wireline broadband providers. Current broadband network providers respond that, given existing market forces, they have neither the incentive nor the ability to constrain independent applications providers, that constraining their ability to manage their networks would discourage their investment in broadband networks, and that municipal networks enjoy an unfair advantage in capital markets.

To date, the debate has proceeded on an abstract level. The purpose of this report is to provide a more concrete discussion of access to wireline broadband networks. To that end, this report provides a discussion of what broadband networks look like; how both consumers and independent applications providers gain access to these networks; and the parameters available to network providers (such as their choices about network architecture, overall bandwidth capacity, bandwidth reserved for their own use, traffic prioritization, the terms and rates for access to their networks and for their retail services) that can affect end users' and independent applications providers' access to those networks.

WHAT DO WIRELINE BROADBAND NETWORKS LOOK LIKE?

The cable and telephone companies' networks are not static; they continue to be upgraded. The various network providers are in different stages of deploying digital IP technology. They are each employing unique network architectures that build off their legacy networks and/or reflect their perceptions of the most cost-effective networks to deploy. Despite these differences, however, each of the networks has three primary components, as shown in figure 1, a schematic representation of a wireline IP broadband network. These three components are the broadband "last mile" grid out to end-user customers; the company's proprietary IP network, with servers for the various applications feeding into a service router that controls the flow of traffic all the way to the customer premise; and the company's facilities in what has traditionally been called the internet backbone (and is sometimes referred to as the "public internet"). The latter connects to independent applications providers, though it is also possible for independent applications providers to connect directly to a broadband network provider's proprietary IP network, as shown in figure 1. Many independent applications providers also have substantial internet facilities. For example, in order to minimize the number of times their content must be handed off from one internet backbone provider to another when responding to an end-user query, these applications providers "cache" their content close to their customers by maintaining multiple servers scattered around the country in which they maintain frequently-updated databases. Since it is possible that congestion could cause delay at any of those handoff points, caching data at multiple servers reduces the risk of service degradation.

The schematic representation in figure 1 may help elucidate a number of policy-related discussions. For example, it may help discussants visualize where and how end users and independent applications providers gain access to the broadband network; where and how congestion occurs that threatens the quality of latency-sensitive services; and how a network provider's capacity, architecture, prioritization, and service offering decisions could affect independent applications providers.

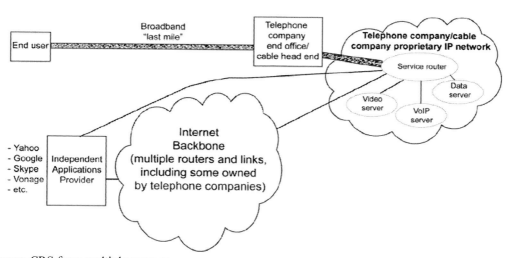

Source: CRS from multiple sources.

Figure 1. Schematic Representation of a Wireline IP Broadband Network.

The Broadband Last Mile

A wireline broadband network provider can choose among various network architectures for its last mile grid. A telephone company can choose to deploy optical fiber from its end office switch all the way to the home, or to the curb, or to a neighborhood node. If it brings the fiber to the curb or to a node, it can then complete the connection to the customer premise by attaching digital subscriber line (DSL) modems to the existing copper line running into the premise. For example, Verizon's Fios service deploys optical fiber all the way to the customer premise, while AT and T's Project Lightspeed deploys fiber to a neighborhood node and then uses existing copper lines and DSL modems to reach the customer.[14] Cable companies most often use hybrid fiber-coaxial cable (HFC) technology, deploying optical fiber from the cable company's head-end facility to a node and using coaxial cable from the node to the end-user premise. The fiber to the home architecture is much more costly to deploy, but can provide substantially more bandwidth than can be provided over a fiber/DSL or HFC last mile[15] and can have its bandwidth expanded more cheaply and easily as demand grows.

If a broadband network provider intends to offer multiple channel video service, it can choose between an architecture that "broadcasts" the signals of all the channels to the end-user premise (the cable company and Verizon approach) and an architecture that transmits to the end user only the particular video channel selected by the customer using her IP set-top box (the "call-up" approach used by AT and T). The "broadcast" approach requires more bandwidth.

Network providers have discretion over several other network parameters. For example, both the telephone and the cable companies have chosen to deploy asymmetric broadband networks that have far more bandwidth for the download of information to end-user customer premises than for the upload of information from end users. This architecture favors the development of applications that are one-to-many or client-server in design. Applications that would require end-user customers to deliver content as quickly as they receive it are limited by asymmetric bandwidth. Asymmetric network architecture supports the cable and telephone companies' triple-play business plans, which focus on end users as receivers, rather than transmitters, of information. This is almost certainly consistent with current demands of most customers. If customer demand were to move toward applications and services requiring more symmetric downloading and uploading capability — perhaps as a result of heightened popularity for interactive games or peer-to-peer distribution of videos and other files — the current asymmetric architecture might constrain the growth of these applications, but it also might create market forces for entry of a third broadband provider with a more symmetric network or for the incumbents to modify their networks to meet the new demand.

A network provider can make other decisions about its last mile network that will affect the bandwidth available to end users. Whether its last mile architecture is all fiber, fiber and copper, or fiber and coaxial cable, it can choose to deploy electronics that determine the bandwidth capacity of the line into the end-user premise. In addition, it can partition the bandwidth capacity of the line into the end-user premise, reserving some portion or portions of the total bandwidth for specific applications. For example, a provider might reserve a portion of the bandwidth for its own applications or for those of an independent applications provider that pays for priority access to the end user.

Each network provider can make its own decisions about these technical parameters, subject to market constraints (though currently not subject to regulatory constraints). For example, Verizon's fiber-to-the-home last mile architecture could potentially provide almost limitless bandwidth if all the fiber strands were "lit," but demand cannot justify the deployment of the electronics needed for such unlimited capacity. As currently configured, Verizon's Fios offering lights just three of the many fiber strands in the optical fiber that comes to the customer premise. These lit strands are called lasers. One of these lasers is reserved for the "broadcast" downloading of all the video channels offered in Verizon's video service. The second laser brings 100 megabits per second (mbps) of bandwidth into the customer premise for downloading packets of all other "incoming" traffic — incoming web pages, e-mails, and other data received as part of internet access service, incoming voice packets, incoming video-on-demand programming,[16] and incoming special services. The third laser is used for uploading packets of all outgoing traffic (associated with these internet access, voice, video-on-demand, and special virtual private network services).

A Verizon end user does not purchase or use the full 100 mbps of bandwidth in the download laser, though that much bandwidth comes into her premise on that laser. Nor does she purchase or use all of the bandwidth in the upload laser. Rather, she purchases specific services that use up to a ceiling level of bandwidth in those lasers. For example, an end user can choose internet access service options with 10, 20, or 30 mbps of downstream bandwidth and with 2 or 5 mbps of upstream bandwidth.[17] The end user also can purchase Verizon's video-on-demand service and/or Verizon's voice service, and have these delivered over the download and upload lasers; or she can purchase an independent applications providers' video-on-demand and/or voice services and have these delivered over the download and upload laser. The remainder of the bandwidth on those lasers — typically 70 mbps of bandwidth on the download laser and substantial bandwidth on the upload laser —are available for special services for that end user. But the end user cannot directly purchase that bandwidth for its own use; rather an independent applications provider that would like to offer a special service to the end user would purchase the bandwidth from Verizon and then recover its costs in its charges to the end user for the service provided over that bandwidth. More specifically, Verizon would require the independent applications provider to purchase an end-to-end connection from its location to the end-user premise. Verizon has characterized these as virtual private network (VPN)-like services that allow the independent applications provider to avoid congestion in the public internet and provide a guaranteed quality of service.

This end-to-end connection is shown in figure 1 by the link that goes directly from the independent applications provider to the service router in the broadband network provider's proprietary IP cloud and then through the broadband last mile to the end user. Although this VPN-like service shares the download and upload lasers with internet access and other services, Verizon is able to manage the traffic on the lasers to assure that the quality of service for that special service is not degraded by other traffic on those lasers (and, as will be discussed below, the special service packets are accorded priority as they are transmitted across servers and links within Verizon's proprietary IP network). Special services that might be provided over such a VPN-like link could range from home monitoring of medical patients by physicians to high definition video streaming. With respect to the services that Verizon itself offers over the three lasers (currently, video, voice, video-on-demand, and internet access services), customers can choose to purchase one or more of the services; discounts are provided for purchasing multiple services. But a Fios customer who does not receive any special VPN-like services could not use the extra bandwidth on the download and upload lasers for its own purposes, such as extra bandwidth for internet access. Nor could an end user who does not purchase Verizon's video service purchase the bandwidth on the video laser for other purposes.

AT and T will be serving most of its Project Lightspeed end-user customers with its last mile network comprised of fiber to the node and a DSL link to the customer premise. The link can provide up to 25 mbps of bandwidth into the premise. Of that bandwidth, 19 mbps currently are reserved for AT and T's video service. Of the remaining 6 mbps of bandwidth, the customer can purchase 1.5 mbps service, 3 mbps service, or 6 mbps service for internet access and voice services. AT and T's proprietary ethernet IP network controls the bandwidth to each premise, based on the level of bandwidth the end user has purchased. AT and T's network is capable of reassigning some of the 19 mbps currently reserved for the proprietary video service to other uses. It would be technically possible for a customer to order additional bandwidth on demand — for example, 10 mbps of bandwidth for three hours for a particular application; this capability is called "turbocharging." But AT and T is concerned that last mile congestion that harms service quality could occur if a household attempted to use AT and T's video service and also an internet application requiring more than 6 mbps of bandwidth at the same time. Therefore AT and T does not currently offer a turbocharge (bandwidth-on-demand) service.

According to CableLabs, the industry research consortium that has developed the Data Over Cable Service Interface Specifications (DOCSIS) that define interface standards for cable modems and supporting equipment, typically a few hundred cable end-user subscribers get internet access by sharing a 6 megahertz (MHz) downstream channel (from the cable network to the customer) and one or more upstream channels (from the customer to the cable network).[18] The downstream channel occupies the space of a single television transmission channel in the cable operator's channel lineup and can provide up to 40 mbps of bandwidth. The cable modems that are most widely deployed in cable networks today (which meet DOCSIS 1.0 and 1.1 specifications) allow upstream channels to deliver up to 10 mbps of bandwidth. Cable companies are now deploying cable modems that meet DOCSIS 2.0 standards that allow upstream channels to deliver up to 30 mbps. DOCSIS 3.0, currently in the late stages of development, will allow several downstream and several upstream channels to be bonded together to multiply the bandwidth delivered to each customer.

Comcast has recently announced that it is rolling out a free feature, called "Powerboost," that will give end users a temporary turbocharge, doubling speeds for many downloads.[19] Comcast currently has one service offering of 6 mbps downstream/384 kbps upstream and a second offering of 8 mbps downstream/768 kbps upstream for internet access and voice service. With the Powerboost feature, customers of these offerings would be able to enjoy downstream speed bursts of 12 and 16 mbps, respectively. The remainder of the bandwidth capacity of the hybrid fiber/coaxial cable lines into their premises would continue to be reserved for video channels. Comcast does not guarantee these speeds for its internet access service. Since many customers share a single channel, the actual speed available to an individual customer at any specific point in time will depend on the level of usage by neighboring customers who share the channel.

Broadband Network Providers' Proprietary IP Networks

As shown in figure 1, independent applications providers can access a broadband network either through the internet backbone or through a direct connection to a service router in the network provider's proprietary IP network.

The broadband network providers are constructing proprietary IP networks that have the intelligence needed to manage overall traffic flow in their networks as well as the flow of traffic to individual end users. Typically, the network providers are deploying these IP networks in each of the metropolitan areas in which they offer service. As shown in figure 1, traffic will arrive at the service router from a number of sources — from the internet backbone, directly from an independent applications provider, or from the network provider's own video, voice, or data server.[20] The service router, communicating with other portions of the proprietary IP network, is programmed to determine the route the incoming traffic will take to reach the end user and to prioritize traffic in order to determine which packets may be delayed or dropped during periods of congestion. This task includes setting the priority algorithm employed at the router to determine which packets are delayed or dropped when congestion occurs. It is possible that a prioritization algorithm could reserve certain links for particular prioritized packets, such that even if there is bandwidth available on those links for non-prioritized packets, such non-prioritized packets cannot be transmitted over those links. For example, as discussed earlier, Verizon has indicated that, as part of its Fios service, a customer can purchase a path or laser that would be dedicated to delivery of a VPN-type end-to-end service, such as a medical monitoring service. Verizon has not clarified whether some of the links —or, at least, some partitioned portion of the bandwidth in those links — would be entirely reserved for such VPN service (denying any other packets access to that bandwidth) or if the packets associated with the VPN service simply would be given the highest priority at the service router, with the bandwidth in those links used for lower priority packets when there are no VPN packets.

The proprietary IP network also manages and controls the traffic flow through the broadband last mile to the end user. It has the intelligence to, among other things, partition the last mile, make available to the end user only the bandwidth purchased by that end user, slow down traffic that may be moving too fast for the bandwidth capability of the last mile, and prioritize traffic moving onto the last mile.[21] Embedded in the proprietary IP network also is the capability to temporarily turbocharge end user lines to accommodate bandwidth-intensive applications or to allow for flexible partitioning of the last mile so that bandwidth that is normally partitioned and reserved for a specific use might be made available to accommodate a different use.[22]

These proprietary IP networks consist of a physical (transmission) network layer, a logical layer (usually the transmission control protocol/internet protocol suite of protocols (often referred to as TCP/IP), which itself consists of several layers), an applications layer, and a content layer.[23] It is technically possible for an independent applications provider to gain access to a broadband network at various layers, with that provider providing more or less of its own intelligence depending on the layer at which access occurs. Some independent applications providers have alleged that they have been denied access at a layer that would allow them to use their own IP capabilities to differentiate their products from those of the network provider — for example, to offer unique filtering services that might be desired by families who want more restrictive program filters than those offered by the broadband network or to offer robustly secure internet service with special intrusion detectors capable of stopping DOS attacks that the broadband network provider might not offer.[24] These independent providers claim that, instead, they were given access only in a fashion that would allow them to resell Verizon's Fios product offering. Verizon responds that, with the advent of its video service, it had to direct data associated with the video service separately from data associated with information service provider (ISP) service, and this required a change in the way it provided independent ISPs access to its network.[25] The independent ISPs question whether such a change was really needed to upgrade the network or whether it was a strategic decision that undermines their ability to differentiate their applications from Verizon's.

The Internet Backbone

As explained in footnote 4, the internet largely consists of a number of routers with links leading into and out of those routers. Traditionally, traffic has traversed the internet based on a best effort standard in which packets are not prioritized, although routers do need some basis for determining which packets to delay or to drop during periods of congestion.

The two largest telephone companies, AT and T and Verizon, are among the largest providers of internet backbone facilities. Other companies with substantial internet backbone companies include Sprint-Nextel, Level3, and Qwest. The cable companies have very limited internet backbone facilities.

There is some question as to whether the telephone companies consider their internet backbone facilities to be part of their proprietary networks, in which they would program their routers to prioritize packets. Referring again to figure 1, AT and T and Verizon have made it clear that they intend to program the service routers in their proprietary IP networks to prioritize incoming packets. But AT and T and Verizon own routers and links in the internet backbone, as well, and they have not clarified whether they intend to program those routers to prioritize packets too.

This distinction could have important public policy implications. If the telephone companies were to, in effect, extend their proprietary IP network into the traditional internet backbone by programming prioritization into their routers in the internet backbone, then if and when congestion occurred at any of the telephone companies' internet backbone routers, non-prioritized packets might be delayed or even dropped. If it were possible and relatively inexpensive to identify the telephone companies as the source of these delayed or dropped packets and to route traffic away from those prioritizing routers, non-telephone company internet backbone providers might be able to expand their capacity and attract customers and traffic away from the telephone companies' internet backbone facilities. But these efforts, if doable, would not be costless. Some independent applications providers — and their customers — could well be harmed by degraded service. (It also is possible that the cable companies, to the extent they use the public internet to offer their applications, could be harmed, since they do not have their own internet backbone facilities.)

If, on the other hand, the telephone companies only prioritized packets once those packets were at the service routers in the telephone companies' private IP networks, then such prioritization is unlikely to degrade the quality of service within the internet backbone itself. Even if the telephone companies chose to focus their investments on their proprietary networks and chose not to upgrade their internet backbone facilities, as long as there continued to be demand for transport over the public internet, then the many non-telephone company providers of internet backbone facilities would still have the incentive to expand and upgrade their internet backbone facilities.

PARAMETERS AVAILABLE TO BROADBAND NETWORK PROVIDERS THAT CAN AFFECT END USERS' AND INDEPENDENT APPLICATIONS PROVIDERS' ACCESS TO THESE NETWORKS

Broadband network providers have many parameters within their control that can affect end users' and independent applications providers' access to these networks. These include:

- the choice of the last-mile network architecture: fiber to the home, fiber to the curb or node (hybrid fiber-DSL), or hybrid fiber-coaxial cable.
- the choice between "broadband" last-mile architecture that transmits all the multiple channel video signals all the way to the end-user premise and "call-up" architecture that only transmits to the end-user premise the particular video channel selected by the customer at the set-top box.
- the choice between more or less symmetry in the network, in terms of bandwidth capacity for an end user to download (receive) a file transmitted over the network vs. bandwidth capacity to upload (send) a file transmitted over the network.
- the choice between deploying a network with very great bandwidth and limited ability to manage traffic congestion (presumably because the bandwidth will be sufficient to minimize congestion) and deploying a network with less bandwidth, but a greater need and ability to manage traffic through prioritization and other capabilities.
- the choice of electronics deployed in the network to turn potential bandwidth capacity into actual available capacity. This includes choices about both the optical fiber strands (lasers) to light and the capability and number of cable or DSL modems deployed.
- the choice of whether and how to partition the bandwidth in both the last-mile connections and the links in the proprietary IP network. This includes choices about how much bandwidth to partition for particular prioritized uses, what those prioritized uses are, and whether the partitioning is flexible (i.e., able to be changed when actual usage patterns result in unused bandwidth in a partitioned portion of a link reserved for prioritized packets while congestion is creating delay or other latency problem for the non-prioritized packets using the non-partitioned portion of the link).
- the choice of where and how to prioritize packets. This includes choices about whether to prioritize packets only within the broadband network provider's proprietary broadband network or also at routers in the internet backbone; what basis to use for delaying individual packets when there is congestion; and what basis to use for dropping individual packets when a router's memory is full.
- the choice of what to include in specific service offerings and the prices for those service offerings. This involves both service offerings to end users and service

offerings to independent applications providers. It includes choices about how many services to bundle together, whether to make services available only as part of a bundle, whether to offer different bandwidth options, what those bandwidth options are, what the prices are for each service offering and option, whether to charge end users or independent applications providers for bandwidth, the price to end users and/or independent applications providers for bandwidth relative to the price of the network provider's end-user service offerings, any usage restrictions in the service offerings for either end users or independent applications providers, the tier or level in the IP network at which independent applications providers gain access, the extent to which an independent applications provider can employ its own IP capability as well as the IP capability in the broadband network to offer service, and the quality of service guarantees in service offerings for independent applications providers.

These parameters are interactive. For example, the greater the bandwidth capacity of the network, the less the need for partitioning or prioritizing traffic or for imposing any use restrictions.

The specific choices that broadband network providers make about these parameters will be driven by several forces — the relative costs of the network architecture options, the actual and perceived demand for (and price sensitivity of) the various service offerings, the actual and potential competition for the provision of both broadband network services and applications, statutory or regulatory constraints (if any), and, to the extent the network providers enjoy some degree of market power, strategic considerations.

HOW MIGHT STRATEGIC BROADBAND NETWORK PROVIDER BEHAVIOR HARM CONSUMERS?

Generally, broadband network providers will not want to take actions that restrict the availability or quality of applications that end users can obtain over their networks. Such restrictive behavior would reduce overall demand for the broadband network and also increase incentives for competitive entry. At the same time, to the extent that the broadband network providers seek to maximize their revenues for what they perceive as the killer broadband applications — voice and video service today, perhaps interactive games or other applications in the future — they will have an incentive to build, operate, and manage their broadband network in a fashion that favors their own applications over competitors' applications. With only limited alternatives to the cable and telephone broadband duopoly for the foreseeable future, and with the cable and telephone companies both pursuing largely the same business plan, the broadband providers might have both the incentive and the ability to exploit their control over access to end users to restrict competition (and the innovation it might bring) and harm consumers. This strategic behavior could occur in several ways.

Given its control over the bandwidth capacity of its network and the partitioning of that bandwidth, if the network provider were to reserve a substantial portion of the bandwidth (in the last-mile network as well as in the links of its proprietary IP network) for its own latency-sensitive services, in order to assure a particular quality of service for those services, that might leave too little bandwidth available for independent applications to assure an equal quality of service for those independent applications. Or there might not be sufficient bandwidth available for multiple independent applications providers to simultaneously serve a single premise or for the provision of certain bandwidth-intensive applications from independent providers.

For example, streaming a high definition television (HDTV) channel currently requires approximately 20 mbps of bandwidth, though advances in compression technology are likely to reduce the required bandwidth to 10 mbps in the near future. If a broadband network provider reserved most of the bandwidth into a customer's premise for its own video service, leaving at most 6 mbps available for the internet access needed to receive independent applications, competitive provision of HDTV would be curtailed. This might, or might not, represent anticompetitive strategic behavior. If the broadband provider has deployed fiber to the home, bringing 100 mbps to the end user premise, and then limits its internet access service offering to 6 mbps, while providing multiple HDTV channels over its own video service, this might suggest an anticompetitive strategic partitioning decision. On the other hand, if the broadband provider has deployed a fiber-DSL hybrid network that only brings 25 mbps to the premise, and its own partitioned video service does not offer HDTV capability (or only limited HDTV capability), then if its internet access service is only 6 mbps, this might reflect network limitations rather than, or as well as, strategic behavior. In either situation, however, if it were technically and economically feasible to partition the bandwidth flexibly, so a customer could use 10 mbps of the bandwidth coming to its premise for either the broadband network's HDTV service offering or an independent application provider's HDTV service offering, the consumer is likely to enjoy greater choice in applications. But even this result is not unambiguous. In a household with multiple high definition television sets, if that household were simultaneously streaming multiple HDTV programs from both the network provider and from an independent provider, flexible partitioning might allow all the programs to be viewed, but not be able to ensure the maintenance of HDTV quality for either program.[26]

Given that the broadband network providers are providers of both end user services and input (network access) services required by their independent applications competitors, they may have the opportunity to set prices for their network access and applications services in a strategic fashion. Consider, for example, the prices that Verizon currently charges its Fios customers for internet access. Verizon offers three options: up to 5 mbps download speed and 2 mbps upstream speed for $34.95, up to 15 mbps download and 2 mbps upload for $49.95, and up to 30 mbps download and 5 mbps upload for $179.95.[27] There are several possible explanations for the huge jump in price for the 30 mbps service. One explanation might be that Verizon would have to incur substantial costs increasing the capacity of its last mile network (and perhaps its proprietary IP network) to handle those bandwidth-intensive applications that would require 30 mbps of download bandwidth. In this case, the high price would accurately reflect actual underlying costs. A second possible explanation might be that the customers with such substantial bandwidth needs tend to be insensitive to price and thus will pay very high prices, or are part of a category of customers (such as business customers) who have traditionally been charged higher rates. Then, the high price would represent a way to perform efficient price discrimination to recover fixed network costs. A third possible explanation might be that Verizon faces potentially strong competition from independent applications providers for the provision of bandwidth-intensive applications, such as HDTV, and by pricing the 30 mbps of internet access service needed for those services at $179.95, while charging a lower prices for its own HDTV or other bandwidth-intensive applications, it could practice strategic behavior that places its competitors in an anticompetitive price squeeze.

More generally, access to the bandwidth provided by broadband networks is a necessary input into the provision of broadband applications. The broadband providers have announced that they seek compensation for such broadband access in two ways — in charges to end users for specific quantities of bandwidth access and in charges to independent applications providers for prioritized access to the broadband network (intended to guarantee service quality, typically comparable to the quality the broadband network providers provide themselves for their own applications). For a particular application, if the difference between the price that the network provider charges end users for its own application service and the "imputed" cost of access to the broadband network that it would have to pay if it were an independent applications provider offering that application (that is, the charges that the network provider imposes on end users and independent applications providers for the bandwidth needed to offer that application) is less than the non-bandwidth-related costs for the network provider to offer that application, then the network provider is placing the independent applications provider in a price squeeze because even if that independent provider were just as efficient as the network provider it would be placed at a competitive disadvantage simply due to the network provider's pricing decisions. This would allow the network provider to succeed in the applications market despite being a less efficient provider.

PROPOSALS FOR GOVERNMENT POLICY ON ACCESS TO BROADBAND NETWORKS

There have been a number of proposals for government policy on access to broadband networks and how best to addressing broadband network providers' strategic behavior.

The FCC Broadband Policy Statement

H.R. 5252, which has been passed by the full House, explicitly authorizes the FCC (at Sec. 201) to enforce the broadband policy statement, and the principles incorporated therein, that the Commission adopted as general principles on August 5, 2005. These principles are:

- consumers are entitled to access the lawful internet content of their choice.
- consumers are entitled to run applications and use services of their choice, subject to the needs of law enforcement.
- consumers are entitled to connect their choice of legal devices that do not harm the network.
- consumers are entitled to competition among network providers, application and service providers, and content providers.

H.R. 5252 explicitly prohibits the FCC from adopting or implementing rules or regulations regarding enforcement of the broadband policy statement, except to adopt procedures for the adjudication of complaints.

These principles are quite general and susceptible to alternative interpretations. They would prohibit a broadband network provider from entirely blocking a particular application, such as a competitor's VoIP service. They do not explicitly prohibit a broadband network provider from prioritizing packets or reserving significant portions of bandwidth for its own applications or for the applications of a preferred independent provider, even if such behavior harmed the quality of service of one or more independent applications providers or effectively precluded independent applications providers from the market. Nor do they explicitly prohibit a broadband network provider from setting charges for network access in a fashion that would place independent applications providers in an anticompetitive price squeeze. Arguably, the fourth principle — consumer entitlement to competition among application and service providers — could be the basis for a complaint against such behavior. No standards are provided, however, for determining what level of competition a consumer is entitled to. For example, the FCC might view the duopoly provision of applications, by the telephone and cable companies, sufficient competition to meet this principle, even if independent applications providers were harmed, or even excluded from the market, by the behavior.

Internet Consumer Bill of Rights

The Internet Consumer Bill of Rights, incorporated in section 903 of H.R. 5252 as amended by the Senate Commerce Committee (originally introduced as S. 2686), requires each internet service provider to allow each subscriber to:

- access and post any lawful content of that subscriber's choosing;
- access any web page of that subscriber's choosing;
- access and run any voice application, software, or service of that subscriber's choosing;
- access and run any video application, software, or service of that subscriber's choosing;
- access and run any search engine of that subscriber's choosing;
- access and run any other application, software, or service of that subscriber's choosing;
- connect any legal device of that subscriber's choosing to the internet access equipment of that subscriber, if such device does not harm the network of the internet service provider; and
- receive clear and conspicuous information, in plain language, about the estimated speeds, capabilities, limitations, and pricing of any internet service offered to the public.

This bill of rights addresses only consumer access to those applications, services, or devices that independent providers are able to offer. If, as a result of a network provider's prioritization, partitioning, and/or pricing decisions, an independent applications provider is not able to offer an application — or can only offer an application that is inferior in quality or higher in price than the competing service offered by the broadband network provider — the independent applications provider has no recourse. The consumer has not been denied access; the provider has been denied access. Arguably, under the Internet Consumer Bill of Rights, a consumer who, because of partitioning, is not allowed to purchase sufficient bandwidth to support the bandwidth-intensive offering of an independent applications provider, but could purchase from her broadband network provider a competing bandwidth-intensive service offering, could bring a complaint that she has been denied access to an application of her choosing. But, unlike the FCC principles, the Internet Consumer Bill of Rights does not include a consumer right to competitive options, and thus cannot address anticompetitive behavior or unfair practices on the part of a broadband network provider.

Network Neutrality

Network neutrality has been a buzz-phrase in the on-going debates, though there is not a single, agreed-upon definition of network neutrality. Indeed, there continue to be questions about what constitutes "neutrality" and to which "networks" such neutrality would apply. For most proponents, network neutrality requires all packets to be treated the same way or, at the least, all packets providing a particular application (such as voice or video) to be treated the same way. Some proponents who would allow for prioritization among applications nonetheless would not allow broadband network providers to charge independent applications providers for such prioritization. Network neutrality proposals include provisions relating to consumer access similar to those found in the FCC principles and Internet Bill of Rights, but in addition have provisions relating to nondiscriminatory or neutral access to broadband networks or the internet by independent applications providers. Three such proposals have been incorporated in legislation introduced in the 109th Congress — the Network Neutrality Act of 2006 (H.R. 5273), the Internet Non-Discrimination Act of 2006 (S. 2360), and the Internet Freedom Preservation Act (S. 2917).

Under H.R. 5273, each broadband network provider has the duty to:

- offer, upon reasonable request to any person, a broadband service for use by such person to offer or access unaffiliated content, applications, and services;
- not discriminate in favor of itself in the allocation, use, or quality of broadband services or interconnection with other broadband networks;
- offer a service such that content, applications, or service providers can offer unaffiliated content, applications, or services in a manner that is at least equal in the speed and quality of service that the operator's content, applications, or service is accessed and offered, and without interference or surcharges on the basis of such content, applications, or services;
- if the broadband network provider prioritizes or offers enhanced quality of service to data of a particular type, prioritize or offer enhanced quality of service to all data of that type (regardless of the origin of such data) without imposing a surcharge or other consideration for such prioritization or quality of service; and
- not install network features, functions, or capabilities that thwart or frustrate compliance with the requirements of objectives of this section.

Under S. 2360, a network operator shall:

- not discriminate in favor of itself or any other person, including any affiliate or company with which such operator has a business relationship, in (A) allocating bandwidth; and (B) transmitting content or applications or services to or from a subscriber in the provision of a communications; ! not assess a charge to any application or service provider not on the network of such operator for the delivery of traffic to any subscriber to the network of such operator;
- offer communications such that a subscriber can access, and a content provider can offer, unaffiliated content or applications or services in the same manner that content of the network operator is accessed and offered, without interference or surcharges;
- treat all data traveling over or on communications in a nondiscriminatory way;
- offer just, reasonable, and nondiscriminatory rates, terms, and conditions on the offering or provision of any service by another person using the transmission component of communications; and
- provide nondiscriminatory access and service to each subscriber.

Under S. 2917, each broadband service provider shall:

- enable any content application, or service made available via the internet to be offered, provided, or posted on a basis that (A) is reasonable and nondiscriminatory, including with respect to quality of service, access, speed, and bandwidth; (B) is at least equivalent to the access, speed, quality of service, and bandwidth that such broadband service provider offers to affiliated content, applications, or services made available via the public Internet into the network of such broadband service provider; and (C) does not impose a charge on the basis of the type of content, applications, or services made available via the internet into the network of such broadband service provider;
- only prioritize content, applications, or services accessed by a user that is made available via the internet within the network of such broadband service provider based on the type of content, applications, or services and the level of service purchased by the user, without charge for such prioritization; and ! not install or utilize network features, functions, or capabilities that impede or hinder compliance with this section.

These three network neutrality proposals have similarities and differences. S. 2360 appears to be the most restrictive. It would prohibit a network provider from prioritizing traffic. Thus, the service router could not be programmed to favor the packets of latency-sensitive applications, such as voice or video service. The proposal also would prohibit a network provider from charging an independent applications provider for the delivery of traffic. All such charges would have to be imposed directly on end users. It also appears to prohibit a network provider from reserving bandwidth for its own, or any other provider's, applications. Referring to figure 1, an independent applications provider could still choose to purchase a direct connection to the service router in the network provider's proprietary IP network, rather than routing its traffic through the internet backbone. But at that service router, all packets would have to be given the exact same priority, whatever the particular type of service that packet was providing, and whether that packet was carrying bits from the network provider's own application, bits from the application of an independent applications provider that had a direct connection to the service router, or bits from the application of an independent service provider that had transmitted those bits through the internet backbone. In addition, neither the links transmitting the packets from the service router to the broadband providers end office/headend nor the last mile connection to the end-user premise could be partitioned in a fashion that would favor the broadband network's applications, for example, by limiting the amount of bandwidth available for independent applications in a way that would not ensure the same quality of service for independent applications and the broadband provider's applications.

H.R. 5273 is less restrictive. It allows the network provider to prioritize traffic — although all traffic for a given application must be assigned the same priority and there can be no surcharge imposed on the higher priority traffic. Referring to figure 1, an independent applications provider could still choose to purchase a direct connection to the service router in the network provider's proprietary IP network, rather than routing its traffic through the internet backbone. At that service router, prioritization could occur, to reduce the risk of delay in packets for latency-sensitive applications, but all packets with bits for a particular type of service (for example, video service) would have to be given the exact same priority, whether those packets were carrying bits from the network provider's own video service, bits from the video service of an independent applications provider that had a direct connection to the service router, or bits from the video service of an independent applications provider that had transmitted those bits through the internet backbone. Like S. 2360, under H.R. 5273, neither the links transmitting the packets from the service router to the broadband providers end office/headend nor the last mile connection to the end-user premise could be partitioned in a fashion that would favor the broadband network's applications, for example, by limiting the amount of bandwidth available for independent applications in a way that would not ensure the same quality of service for independent applications and the broadband provider's applications. Also like S. 2360, H.R. 5273 would prohibit a network provider from charging an independent applications provider for the delivery of traffic. All such charges would have to be imposed directly on end users.

The current network configurations and service offerings of Verizon, AT and T, and Comcast would not appear to meet the requirements in these two network neutrality proposals because they all reserve significant bandwidth for their own video services and do not appear to make an equal amount of bandwidth available for other applications providers. Also, to the extent that these broadband networks incorporate partitioning and prioritization, and charge accordingly, they do not conform with all the network neutrality requirements.

But partitioning and prioritization need not have discriminatory or anticompetitive consequences. For example, the current Fios offering, which brings 100 mbps of bandwidth to a customer premise on a download laser, and offers up to 30 mbps of that bandwidth for downloading any service, appears to make available enough bandwidth for independent applications providers to be able to compete with Verizon's applications in the provision of even bandwidth-intensive applications.

It is not clear how the network neutrality conditions would address a price squeeze. On one hand, the prohibition on surcharges for prioritization or for network access would appear to constrain the ability of a network provider to use charges imposed on independent applications providers to create a price squeeze. On the other hand, there does not appear to be any constraint on the price that end users can be charged for internet access, and if the price of the network provider's applications do not cover the imputed cost of such access plus the other costs of offering the service, the network provider could create an anticompetitive price squeeze.

S. 2917 appears to have an additional point of departure that might result in virtually no restrictions on broadband providers. The duties of broadband service providers outlined in sections 12(a)(4) and (5) apply to "service made available via the Internet," without further delineation. But there may be differences of opinion about which services are offered via the internet. Consider, for example, the VPN-like services available as part of Verizon's Fios offering, discussed earlier. Those services would be provided by independent applications providers that would purchase the bandwidth from Verizon in order to have an end-to-end connection with the end user; the independent applications provider who purchases that bandwidth would be compensated by charging the end user for the service provided. This end-to-end connection is shown in figure 1 by the link that goes directly from the independent applications provider to the service router in the broadband network provider's proprietary IP cloud and then through the broadband last mile to the end user. Arguably, since the traffic transported over this VPN service never touches the public internet, but rather goes from an independent applications provider directly to Verizon's proprietary IP network over a private line connection, it is not "a service made available via the Internet." With that interpretation, services offered over this VPN path would not be subject to the nondiscrimination provisions relating to prioritization, partitioning, and charges in sections 12(a)(4) and (5).

More significantly, as shown in figure 1, the broadband network providers' video services do not use the public internet; they receive satellite, terrestrial, or broadcast feeds into their video server and then route those signals through the service router in their proprietary IP networks and then through their last mile networks to subscribers. The nondiscriminatory bandwidth and prioritization provisions in section 12(a)(4) and (5) therefore may not apply to the network providers' video services or any other applications that are not delivered through the public internet.

Antitrust and Unfair Methods of Competition Laws

There have been several proposals that anticompetitive broadband network access behavior be addressed through application of existing or modified antitrust and competition laws.

The Internet Freedom and Nondiscrimination Act of 2006 (H.R. 5417), which has been ordered to be reported out of the House Judiciary Committee, would amend the Clayton Act by inserting a new section 28 making it unlawful for any broadband network provider:

- to fail to provide its broadband network services on reasonable and nondiscriminatory terms and conditions such that any person can offer or provide content, applications, or services to or over the network in a manner that is at least equal to the manner in which the provider or its affiliates offer content, applications, and services, free of any surcharge on the basis of the content, application, or service;

- to refuse to interconnect its facilities with the facilities of another provider of broadband network services on reasonable and nondiscriminatory terms and conditions;
- to block, to impair, to discriminate against, or to interfere with the ability of any person to use a broadband network service to access, to use, to send, to receive, or to offer lawful content, applications, or services over the Internet;
- to impose an additional charge to avoid any conduct that is prohibited by this subsection;
- to prohibit a user from attaching or using a device on the provider's network that does not physically damage or materially degrade other users' utilization of the network; or
- to fail to clearly and conspicuously disclose to users, in plain language, accurate information concerning any terms, conditions, or limitations on the broadband network service.

In addition, under H.R. 5417, if a broadband network provider prioritizes or offers enhanced quality of service to data of a particular type, it must prioritize or offer enhanced quality of service to all data of that type (regardless of the origin or ownership of such data) without imposing a surcharge or other consideration for such prioritization or enhanced quality of service.

Since enforcement of the Clayton Act is solely within the jurisdiction of either the Federal Trade Commission (FTC) or the Antitrust Division of the Department of Justice (DOJ), the general thrust of H.R. 5417 is to implement the network neutrality provisions in H.R. 5273, but to move enforcement responsibility from the FCC to the antitrust agencies, which specialize in competition analysis and, in the case of the FTC, consumer protection analysis. The FTC has indicated that it believes it already possesses sufficient authority to adequately address the competition and consumer protection issues of concern to network neutrality proponents,[28] but "any new legislation should clearly preserve the FTC's existing authority over activities currently within its jurisdiction."[29]

H.R. 5417 also would have the effect of creating a private right of action by aggrieved applications providers. Although H.R. 5417 contains no explicit language to that effect, section 4(a) of the Clayton Act[30] authorizes treble-damage suits in appropriate district courts by "any person who shall be injured in his business or property by reason of anything forbidden in the antitrust laws...."

The Digital Age Communications Act of 2005 (S. 2113), which is based in large part on a proposal developed as part of the Digital Age Communications Act (DACA) project of the Progress and Freedom Foundation,[31] would replace the current regulatory framework with a framework based on the Federal Trade Commission Act (15 U.S.C. 41 et seq.). It would prohibit unfair methods of competition, and give the FCC the authority to enforce the law. Specifically:

- it shall be unlawful for any provider of electronic communication service to engage or participate, or attempt to engage or participate, in unfair methods of competition, or unfair or deceptive practices in or affecting electronic communications networks and electronic communications services;

- the FCC may, by rule, define with specificity, the acts or practices that shall constitute unfair methods of competition or unfair or deceptive acts or practices;
- promulgated rules may include such requirements as the FCC determines necessary to prevent any methods, acts, or practices prohibited by this section;
- the FCC shall have no authority to issue rules that declare unlawful an act or practice on the grounds that such act or practice is an unfair method of competition or unfair or deceptive act or practice, except that the FCC may declare an act or practice unlawful if the FCC determines, based on a showing of clear and convincing evidence presented in a rulemaking proceeding that (i) marketplace competition is not sufficient to adequately protect consumer welfare, and (ii) such act or practice (I) causes or is likely to cause substantial injury to consumers, and (II) is not avoidable by consumers themselves and not outweighed by countervailing benefits to consumers or to competition;
- the FCC shall have authority to hear complaints from any party injured by a violation of the prohibitions established and to award damages to such injured party if the FCC determines that a violation has occurred.

Although these provisions lack specificity as to what types of behavior would represent unfair methods of competition or unfair or deceptive practices, and in particular do not provide any specificity about discriminatory practices, they do potentially provide a procedure for independent applications providers to file complaints about the terms, conditions, and prices under which they have access to a broadband provider's network. The effectiveness of such a complaint procedure, however, may depend on the standard used in determining whether a particular act or practice represents a legal violation.

On May 10, 2006, in response to questions after his keynote speech at an American Enterprise Institute conference on Key Issues in Telecommunications Policy, Alfred Kahn, who was a DACA Project Advisory Committee Member, commented on the DACA proposal incorporated in S. 2113.[32] He stated that he agreed with the overall framework, but that he believed the proposed standard for finding a violation was set too high. He suggested the standard for a finding of unfair methods of competition or unfair competitive practices should be based solely on demonstrated harm to consumers. He voiced concern with the methodology frequently employed in antitrust analysis today that assumes that no intervention is needed if it can be shown that each $1 loss in consumer surplus is matched by a $1 gain in producer surplus. He argued that unfair practices laws are intended to protect consumers, even if there might be some negative impact on producer efficiency. He therefore would want unfair methods of competition to be "close to *per se* illegal."

REFERENCES

[1] See George Ford, Thomas Koutsky, and Lawrence Spiwack, "Competition After Unbundling: Entry, Industry Structure and Convergence," Phoenix Center Policy Paper Number 21, July 2005, available at [http://www.phoenix-center.org/pcpp/PCPP21Final.pdf], viewed on May 24, 2006.

[2]   According to the most recent FCC report, *High-Speed Services for Internet Access: Status as of June 30, 2005,* April 2006, at table 6, the vast preponderance of high-speed internet access lines were provided by local telephone companies or cable companies: of the 42.9 million total high-speed line (over 200 kilobits per second (kbps) in at least one direction) in the U.S. in June 2005, 14.3 million were provided by Regional Bell Operating Companies, 2.3 million were provided by other incumbent telephone companies, and 23.9 million were provided via cable modems. Tables 3 and 6 of that report indicate that of the 38.5 million high-speed lines designed to serve primarily residential end users, 61.0% used cable modems and 37.2% were asymmetric digital subscriber lines (ADSL), and that the vast majority of the latter were provided by local telephone companies.

[3]   See, for example, Robert D. Atkinson and Philip J. Weiser, "A 'Third Way' on Network Neutrality," The Information Technology and Innovation Foundation, May 30, 2006, at pp. 7-8, available at [http://www.innovationpolicy.org/pdf/netneutrality.pdf], viewed on May 31, 2006.

[4]   Latency is affected by physical distance, the number of "hops" from one internet network to another internet network that must be made to deliver the packets (since there can be congestion at each hand-off point), and voice-to-data conversion. Congestion that delays the transmission of packets can cause several problems. (The following is a distillation of a description for lay readers presented by Ed Felten in [http://www.freedom-to-tinker.com?p=983]   and   [http://www.freedom-to-tinker.com/?p=986], both viewed on May 24, 2006.) In effect, the internet (or a proprietary IP network) is as a set of routers connected by links. Packets of data get passed from one router to another, via links. A packet is forwarded from router to router, until it arrives at its destination. Typically, each router has several incoming links on which packets arrive, and several outgoing links on which it can send packets. When a packet shows up on an incoming link, the router will figure out on which outgoing link the packet should be forwarded. If that outgoing link is free, the packet can be sent out on it immediately. But if the outgoing link is busy transmitting another packet, the newly arrived packet will have to wait — it will be "buffered" in the router's memory, waiting its turn until the outgoing link is free. Buffering lets the router deal with temporary surges in traffic. The router will be programmed to determine which packets should be delayed and also, when the link is available, which buffered packet should be transmitted. That is, a packet prioritization scheme is devised. This could be a simple, first-in, first-out scheme or a favor-applications-sensitive-to-packet-delay scheme, or a pay-for-priority scheme, or something else. But if packets keep showing up faster than they can be sent out on some outgoing link, the number of buffered packets will grow and grow, and eventually the router will run out of buffer memory. At that point, if one more packet shows up, the router has no choice but to discard a packet. It can discard the newly arriving packet, or it can make room for the new packet by discarding something else. But something has to be discarded. The router will be programmed to determine which packets should be dropped, thus creating a second packet prioritization scheme. Again, this could be a simple, first-in, first-out scheme or a favor-applications-sensitive-to-dropped-packets scheme, or a pay-for-priority scheme, or something else. Dropped packets can be retransmitted, but for those applications, such as voice, that require the packets to arrive and be reassembled within

a short period of time, such packet recovery might not occur in the timely fashion needed to retain service quality. With such congestion, at least two problems may occur. One problem is dropped packets. Some applications are more sensitive than others to dropped packets. A second problem is "jitter" caused by the delay of certain packets. Internet traffic is usually "bursty," with periods of relatively low activity punctuated by occasional bursts of packets. (For example, browsing the Web generates little or no traffic while reading the page, but a burst of traffic when the browser needs to fetch a new page.) Even if the router is programmed to minimize delay by only delaying low-priority packets when congestion absolutely requires such delay, if the high-priority traffic is bursty, then low-priority traffic will usually move through the network with little delay, but will experience noticeable delay whenever there is a burst of high-priority traffic. This on-again, off-again delay is called jitter. Jitter has no affect when downloading a big file, for which one's concern is the average packet arrival rate rather than arrival time of a particular packet. But the quality of applications like voice conferencing or VoIP — which rely on steady streaming of interactive, realtime communication — can suffer a lot if there is jitter.

[5]   For simplification of exposition, this report will refer to those applications that are sensitive to dropped packets or to jitter or any other congestion-related transmission problem as "latency-sensitive" applications.

[6]   "P2P in 2005," Presentation by Andrew Parker, co-founder and chief technology officer, CacheLogic, available at [http://www.cachelogic.com/research/ 2005_ slide01.php], viewed on June 9, 2006.

[7]   See Julie Bosman and Tom Zeller Jr., "Warner Bros. To Sell Movies and TV Shows on Internet," *New York Times*, May 9, 2006, at p. C3.

[8]   See the discussion below in the section entitled "What Do Wireline Broadband Networks Look Like?"

[9]   Customer churn is the number of customers who discontinue purchasing service from a provider within a period of time. It is typically measured as the churn rate — the percentage of customers who discontinue service during a period of time.

[10]   *In the Matter of Inquiry Concerning High-Speed Access to the Internet Over Cable and Other Facilities; Internet Over Cable Declaratory Ruling; Appropriate Regulatory Treatment for Broadband Access to the Internet Over Cable Facilities,* 17 FCC Rcd. 4798, 4799 (March 15, 2002). In this decision, the FCC concluded that the telecommunications functionality in cable modem service is integral to the service, and not transparent to the consumer, and therefore cable modem service should be treated as a pure information service and not subject to the requirements imposed on telecommunications services under Title II of the Communications Act (47 U.S.C. 151 *et seq.*).

[11]   *National Cable and Telecommunications Association v. Brand X Internet Services,* 125 S.Ct. 2688 (2005).

[12]   *In the Matter of Appropriate Framework for Broadband Access to the Internet Over Wireline Facilities,* Report and Order and Notice of Proposed Rulemaking, 20 FCC Rcd. 14853 (September 23, 2005). The FCC used the same argument to support its DSL decision as it used in its cable modem decision. Not surprisingly, the United Power Line Council has petitioned the FCC to issue a declaratory ruling that broadband over power lines is an information service akin to cable modem and DSL service. (*In the*

Matter of the Petition of the United Power Line Council for a Declaratory Ruling Regarding the Classification of Broadband over Power Line Internet Access Service as an Information Service, Petition for Declaratory Ruling, filed December 23, 2005, available at [http://www.uplc.utc.org/file_depot/0-10000000/0-10000/7966/conman/ Petition+for+De claratory+Ruling.pdf]

[13] For example, at the November 10, 2005, panel of academics at the "Peripheral Visionaries' VoIP Communications Policy Summit" conference sponsored by pulver.com, Susan Crawford of Cardozo Law School, argued that it is unlikely to be possible to craft legislative language that broadband network providers could not get around in the name of network management, and that instead the public policy focus should be on the "real problem" of lack of competitive alternatives to the cable and telephone networks.

[14] AT and T has indicated that, as it builds out its Lightspeed network, it may serve those customers in new housing developments under construction by deploying optical fiber all the way to their premises. These may represent as many as 5% of AT and T customers.

[15] The actual amount of bandwidth provided by fiber, fiber/copper, or HFC will depend on a number of factors, including how much of the optical fiber is "lit" by electronics and the type of modems used.

[16] Verizon's video-on-demand service is provided separately from the rest of its multichannel video service offering because video-on-demand requires communication between the end user and the video-on-demand server in Verizon's proprietary IP network to call up the specific program from the thousands of programs available, whereas the multi-channel video service simply "broadcasts" all the channels in the service to the end-user premise, with no need for prior communication from the end user.

[17] The pricing of these options are discussed below in the section entitled How Might Strategic Broadband Network Provider Behavior Harm Consumers?

[18] See "DOCSIS Project Primer," a document prepared by the CableLabs consortium and last updated September 30, 2005, available at [http://www.cablemodem.com/primer/], viewed on June 6, 2006.

[19] See, for example, Dionne Searcey and Sarmad Ali, "Comcast to Speed Downloads to Some Movie, Music Files," *The Wall Street Journal*, June 1, 2006, at p. D3.

[20] For ease of presentation, the schematic diagram in figure 1 does not attempt to show every link into a broadband network. The voice, data, and video servers are each shown in the diagram with only a link to the service router, but each of these applications servers will also have other links to the sources of voice, data, and video information transmitted. For example, the video server will be connected (by satellite, terrestrial, and broadcast connections) to the sources of the video programming provided by the network provider.Similarly, since lots of voice traffic continues to flow over the traditional public switched telephone network (PSTN), there will continue to be traffic that comes from the PSTN directly into the telephone company's end office in analog format, but that traffic may then be digitized and routed by the telephone company's proprietary IP network.

[21] Prioritization may play an important network management role as peer-to-peer (P2P) applications become more common. One characteristic of P2P networking is to

distribute files as broadly through the network as possible, rather than maintaining files at central servers, so that files can be obtained quickly and with less risk from failure at a single mode. Many P2P applications are constructed to identify all the places where a particular file is located, identify which of those places are served by significant uploading bandwidth, and then obtain the file from those locations. These applications tend to place a burden on last mile networks and proprietary IP networks with large upload capacity. But increasing bandwidth capacity at those locations where P2P applications are creating congestion only creates the feedback effect of making those locations even more attractive for P2P applications. One solution that has been proposed by broadband network providers is for the network manager to be able to employ prioritization in a fashion that slows down P2P packets in order to allow other traffic to flow at these P2P-created congestion points and to discourage the cycle of increases in upload bandwidth intended to reduce congestion automatically attracting additional P2P traffic that creates new congestion. This would help broadband providers manage their networks. But it might diminish efficiencies of P2P networking. Such prioritization is inconsistent with one of the fundamental principles articulated by most proponents of "network neutrality" — that all packets should be treated the same, or that, at the least, all packets associated with the same type of application should be treated the same.

[22] Not every proprietary IP network will necessarily have these capabilities, but announcements by the various broadband network providers suggest that such capabilities are technically possible.

[23] See, for example, Richard S. Whitt, "A Horizontal Leap Forward: Formulating a New Communications Public Policy Framework Based on the Network Layers Model," 56 *Federal Communications Law Journal* 587 (2004).

[24] See Louis Trager, "ISPs Accuse Verizon of Double-Cross on FiOS Wholesaling," *Communications Daily*, November 3, 2005.

[25] Untitled article, *Communications Daily*, November 8, 2005, at p. 8.

[26] But this does highlight how partitioning places constraints on the end user's ability to receive multiple HDTV programs simultaneously from one or more independent applications providers, even if that end user has purchased a bundled service offering with total bandwidth capable of providing multiple HDTV programs simultaneously.

[27] These were the service and price options listed on Verizon's website, on June 22, 2006, for those residential households located in Fairfax County, VA for whom Verizon's Fios service was available.

[28] Behavior that is unfairly discriminatory or anticompetitive is reachable via sections 1 or 2 of the Sherman Act (15 U.S.C. 1and 2, which prohibit, respectively, contracts or conspiracies in restraint of trade and monopolization), or as a violation of section 5 of the FTC Act (15 U.S.C. 45(a), which proscribes "unfair methods of competition" or "unfair or deceptive acts or practices"). The Sherman Act is enforceable by either the FTC or the DOJ; the FTC Act is enforceable only by the FTC..

[29] "FTC Jurisdiction Over Broadband Internet Access Services," Testimony of FTC Commissioner William E. Kovacic before the Senate Judiciary Committee, Hearing on Reconsidering Our Communications Laws: Ensuring Competition and Innovation, June 14, 2006, available at [http://judiciary.senate.gov/print_testimony.cfm?id=1937 and wit_id=5415], viewed on August 31, 2006.

[30] 15 U.S.C. 15(a).

[31] Digital Age Communications Act: Proposal of the Regulatory Framework Working Group of the Digital Age Communications Act Project of the Progress and Freedom Foundation, June 5, 2005, available at [http://www.pff.org/issues-pubs/other/050617regframework.pdf], viewed on June 21, 2006.

[32] Alfred Kahn, keynote address and response to questions, American Enterprise Institute conference on Key Issues in Telecommunications Policy, Washington, DC, May 10, 2006.

In: Broadband Internet: Access, Regulation and Policy   ISBN: 978-1-60456-073-2
Editor: Ellen S. Cohen, pp. 27-49   © 2007 Nova Science Publishers, Inc.

Chapter 2

BUNDLING RESIDENTIAL TELEPHONE, INTERNET, AND VIDEO SERVICES : ISSUES FOR CONGRESS[*]

Charles B. Goldfarb
Industrial Organization and Telecommunications Resources,
Science, and Industry Division

ABSTRACT

Technological advances and deregulatory actions now allow consumers to obtain their local and long distance telephone services, their high-speed Internet services, and their video services from competing technologies . The convergence of previously distinct markets has required companies to seek strategies for holding on to their traditional customers while seeking new ones . One of those strategies is for companies to offer bundles of "traditional" and "new" services at a single price that often represents a discount off the sum of the prices of the individual services . These bundled service offerings are favored by many consumers . They provide the convenience of "one stop shopping" and in some situations, by providing the full panoply of services at a fixed price, make it easier for consumers to comparison shop . They also are favored by many providers because they tend to reduce "churn" - the rate at which customers shift to competitors - and allow providers to exploit economies of scope in marketing .

But bundling also can create public policy issues for Congress . The bundled offerings typically provide some combination of interstate telecommunications services, intrastate telecommunications services, and non-telecommunications services (information services, video services, and even customer premises equipment) for a single price . The federal Universal Service Fund - the federal subsidy program that assures affordable telephone rates for high-cost (rural) and low-income telephone customers as well as for schools, libraries, and rural health facilities - is supported by an assessment on interstate telecommunications revenues only. But it is difficult to identify the portion of revenues generated by a bundled service offering attributable to the interstate telecommunications portion of that bundle. There is no unambiguous way for providers to assign a portion of the bundled price to interstate telecommunications services or for fund administrators to audit that assignment. In addition, some taxes are

---

[*] Excerpted from CRS Report RL32232, dated February 17, 2004.

assessed upon one or more, but not all, of the services included in various bundled service offerings . This creates the same assessment and auditing problem for these taxes as exists for the federal Universal Service Fund. This has important policy implications at a time when many Members of Congress seek to shelter Internet services-which often are included in these bundles- from taxation without placing any group of providers at a competitive advantage or disadvantage .

Some observers have been concerned that bundled service offerings could have anticompetitive consequences if they foster industry consolidation or if a provider has market power for one of the services in its bundled offering and can use that offering to tie that service to a competitive service in a fashion that reduces competition for the competitive service .

Leaders in both the House and the Senate Commerce Committees have announced that in the 109" Congress they plan to review and reform the 1996 Telecommunications Act (P.L .104-104) in light of the market convergence that underlies the trend toward bundling . This report will be updated as events warrant .

Technological advances and deregulatory actions now allow consumers to obtain their local and long distance telephone services, their high-speed Internet services, and their video services from competing technologies . Companies that in the past sold a narrow suite of services in relative insulation from competition now are actively entering new service markets and also facing entry by others into their traditional markets . The convergence of previously distinct markets has required companies to seek strategies for holding on to their traditional customers while seeking new ones. One of those strategies is for companies to offer bundles of their "traditional" services and "new" services - typically at a single price that represents a discount off the sum of the prices of the individual services .

Today, most incumbent local exchange carriers ("ILECs"),[1] competitive local exchange carriers ("CLECs"),[2] wireless carriers, cable companies, and satellite television companies have bundled service offerings that compete, to varying degrees, with one another .

Leaders in both the House and the Senate Commerce Committees have announced that in the 109' Congress they plan to review and reform the 1996 Telecommunications Act (P.L . 104-104) in light of the market convergence that underlies the trend toward bundling.[3]

THE MARKET FORCES DRIVING BUNDLING

The trend toward bundled service offerings is driven by both demand and supply .

Bundled service offerings are favored by many consumers. They provide the convenience of "one stop shopping" and, to the extent that competitors' packages include the same (or a very similar) bundle of services, can make it easier for consumers to comparison shop, calculate their total telecommunications and media expenditures, and switch from one provider to another by switching just a single account.[4]

According to J.D. Power and Associates,[5] the share of households that report bundling at least their local and long distance services with one carrier has increased from 26% in 2002 to 40% in 2003, an overall increase of more than 10 million households, and customers who bundle services report higher overall satisfaction than those who are not bundling services . The Yankee Group made a similar finding - even though bundles have only been available in many parts of the country within the past year, a third of Americans already receive long distance and local service from the same company.[6] According to Wayne Huyard, president of MCI's mass markets division, half of MCI's consumer-side revenues comes .from the 3.5 million customers of its bundled service and that proportion is expected to increase to 75% by 2005.[7]

But the bundling phenomenon extends far beyond the simple packaging of local and long distance telephone services, and is driven by providers as much as by consumers. Although bundled offerings can make comparison shopping easier, they also tend to foster customer loyalty, thereby reducing "churn" - the rate at which customers discontinue service (in order to shift to competitors) . They also allow providers to exploit marketing economies of scope. As providers enter new markets, they can market both their traditional services and their new services with a consolidated sales and marketing force and campaign.

Until recently, most households had no alternative to their local exchange carrier for local telephone service and no alternative to their local cable system for subscription video service. The ILECs and cable systems enjoyed relatively stable relationships with their customers. Customer chum was extremely low because in most situations there were government-imposed prohibitions on other providers offering competitive service, leaving customers with no alternative providers to turn to. But today, CLECs, wireless carriers, and cable systems offer local telephone service in competition with the ILECs, and satellite systems offer subscription video service in competition with cable systems . TI ,FCs and cable systems now face rising levels of customer chum,[8] analogous to what AT and T and its long distance competitors have experienced with their customers since MCI, Sprint, and a host of smaller facilities-based carriers and resellers entered the long distance market in the 1980s, and what the wireless carriers have begun to experience as well.[9] Competitive entry and market convergence have increased the chum rate for all providers .

The costs associated with customer chum are substantial . Providers face up-front costs to capture and serve a customer . To serve that customer profitably, the provider must recover these costs before the customer changes provider. These costs include the acquisition (marketing and sales) costs associated with gaining new customers, retaining existing customers, and winning back customers who leave for another provider. They also include costs associated with connecting the customer to the provider's network and activating service-providing the wireline or wireless connection, incorporating customer data in the provider's operating support systems, sometimes placing equipment on customer premises, etc . If the provider faces high churn rates, absent a substantial initial customer charge (such as a connection charge), it may fail to fully recover these up-front costs . One industry analyst has estimated that wireless providers have per customer acquisition costs of $ 150 to $300 and payback cycles as long as 14 months.[10] Another industry analyst estimates residential wireless per customer acquisition costs of $300 to $425.[11] But the wireless industry has annual customer churn rates in the vicinity of 30%, which are expected to grow with the recent implementation of local number portability.[12] Thus, analysts say wireless carriers currently are not able to fully recover their acquisition costs for a substantial portion of customers . The same is true for other telecom, Internet, and video service providers.[13]The higher the churn rate, the less likely providers will be able to fully recover their up-front costs from each customer - at the same time that pressure is placed on providers to increase their efforts (and costs) for acquiring and retaining customers.[14]The high costs associated with churn have spawned an industry of market researchers to help firms identify customer purchasing patterns and construct strategies for minimizing chum.[15] According to these market researchers, increasing the number of services included in the bundle tends to reduce churn.[16] Bundled service offerings therefore tend to provide an advantageous strategy for large companies that are able to offer a broad array of services .

Verizon has announced that the company plans to offer consumers as many services as possible in its bundled offerings, with traditional voice options supplemented by wireless, video services, and high-speed Internet ; according to Jill Wagner, Verizon vice president of consumer marketing, "It's not just the [local companies] and the long distance providers . You have to throw in the six wireless providers, and you have to throw in the cable companies . That's the market."[17] BellSouth has the same perspective. Lisa Fox, BellSouth's director of consumer marketing, has stated: "Because we can sell them local, long distance, data, wireless and - soon - video all on one bill, that's really proved to be a good retention tool for us. Customers can't find that in our region with anyone else today." [18]

As these large bundled service offerings have grown in popularity, companies with narrower capabilities that have traditionally offered stand-alone services have had to partner with larger companies in order to participate in a market environment that favors bundling.[19]

Since identical bundled offerings facilitate comparison shopping, providers have a strong incentive to differentiate or distinguish their bundled service offerings from their competitors' offerings . Otherwise, their primary way to hold on to customers is to keep cutting prices . The best way to differentiate a bundle is to include a service that competitors either cannot offer at all or cannot offer at the same quality, cost, or convenience .

WIRELINE-OF BUNDLING STRATEGIES

Most wireline providers - ILECs and CLECs - offer bundled local and long distance telephone services. Unadorned by special features, long distance service and (increasingly now) local service have become commodities, subject to fierce price competition and high churn levels.[20] Although many CLECs initially attempted to enter the residential market by using their own network facilities or by reselling the ILECs' retail products, in almost all cases CLECs have abandoned those approaches as not competitively viable . Instead, most CLECs provide residential local service by leasing network facilities from the ILECs, in particular by leasing the unbundled network element ("UNE") known as UNE-platform or UNE-P,[21] under terms set out in the 1996 Telecommunications Act, as implemented by the FCC and state public service commissions.[22] One group of CLECs has estimated that in the second quarter of 2003 80% of all residential local service offered by CLECs as part of bundled service offerings was provided using UNE-P leased from the Regional Bell Operating Companies ("RBOCs")[23]. Some ILECs have attempted to differentiate their bundled offerings from CLECs by including vertical features such as voice mail and privacy management (to block telemarketers) that are not part of the UNE-P they are required to provide to CLECs but that CLECs are unlikely to be able to offer at equal quality or cost on their own.[24]

Another way that ILECs attempt to differentiate their bundled service offerings from CLEC offerings is to offer high-speed Internet access service by using DSL technology to provide both voice and data services over the existing copper telephone lines. Although in many geographic locations it is not feasible for CLECs to deploy their own DSL equipment to serve residential customers,[25] the DSL equipment is not available as a UNE, nor as part of the UNE-P . As a result, in many geographic areas, CLECs do not, themselves, offer bundled voice and DSL service . Even Covad, which specializes as a provider of high-speed Internet access and continues to expand its footprint, will have collocated DSL equipment in only 2,000 (out of more than 10,000) ILEC central offices by mid-2004, and will be able to reach somewhat less than half (under 50 million) of U .S. households[26]. Most residential customers seeking to receive both voice service and high-speed Internet access service over their telephone lines have the following choices : to receive both voice and Internet access service from their ILEC; to receive voice service from their ILEC and high-speed Internet service from a provider such as Covad, with that Internet service provider collocating its own DSL equipment in the 11,EC's network and leasing the data portion of the ILEC line serving that customer at negotiated prices that need not reflect costs;[27] or to receive the two services through a "line splitting" arrangement[28] under which a CLEC that specializes in offering high-speed Internet access (data) service, and another CLEC that specializes in offering voice services, could jointly use the unbundled loop to provide the customer both voice and Internet access services. This last option has allowed some CLECs, including AT and T and MCI, to respond to the ILECs' bundled local/long distance/high-speed Internet access offerings by entering into contractual marketing relationships with Covad, to offer a similar bundled service. But it is more complex - and more expensive - to coordinate line splitting than for an ILEC to offer the two services using its own facilities .

According to a December 5, 2003 SBC press release,[29]
Long distance and DSL help [SBC] reduce [its] chum:

- Adding long distance to an access line reduces the company's chum rate by 9 percent. Churn drops by 61 percent when a DSL line is added to an SBC bundle.
- Together, long distance and DSL reduce chum by 73 percent.

WIRELINE, WIRELESS, VIDEO BUNDLING STRATEGIES

Today, bundled offerings have expanded far beyond the telephone and high-speed Internet access services traditionally offered by ILECs and CLECs, to include video and wireless services as well. Initially, each provider's bundles tended to be limited to the combination of services that could readily be provided by the firm's underlying network technology, and thus each provider tended to offer different combinations of services . Traditional circuit-switched public telephone networks, coaxial cable television networks, wireless networks, Internet protocol networks, and satellite systems each have their advantages and limitations with respect to services offered . To minimize market fallout from the limitations of their chosen technologies, however, providers increasingly are teaming with companies that have different underlying network technologies in order to provide complete bundled offerings .

For example, the incumbent local telephone companies have been able to quickly enter the long distance market as soon as they received government approval to do so.[30] Verizon already serves 15 .9 million long distance customers, SBC 11.5 million, and BellSouth 3.4 million.[31] But to date it has not proved viable for local telephone companies to use their circuit-switched telephone networks to offer video services. Instead, in order to compete with the bundled offerings of cable operators, many ILECs are entering into partnership arrangements with satellite companies to market satellite television services as part of a telephone company bundled offering . Both Verizon and BellSouth have entered into marketing agreements with DirecTV to begin offering subscription video services as part of their bundled service offerings in 2004[32]. Similarly, SBC has entered into a co-branding deal with Echostar, also beginning in 2004, to offer "SBC Dish Network.[33]

Similarly, local cable television systems' fiber optic platforms have helped cable companies become the largest providers of high-speed Internet access (through the use of cable modems) . As of September 30, 2003, 15 million cable customers received cable modem service.[34] But many cable systems have not yet made the network upgrades needed to offer telephone services ; as of September 30, 2003, there were 2.5 million residential cable telephony customers in the United States.[35] Recently, however, a number of cable systems have announced that rather than undertake the expensive investment needed to upgrade their coaxial cable networks to provide telephone service - and have to continue to pay high access charges to the 11 FCs to terminate calls - they plan to use Internet Protocol technology to offer voice services, in some cases jointly with long distance carriers.[36] Cable companies have undertaken this bundling strategy at least in part as a customer retention strategy against the satellite companies.[37] Similarly, some cable companies are deploying video-on-demand service to capture and maintain customers.[38]

According to Jeffrey Halpern, an analyst at Sanford C. Bernstein and Co,[39] wireless is the key to distinguishing phone companies from their cable television rivals, many of which have phone and Internet access packages but don't have wireless offerings . The ILECs that have wireless joint ventures (SBC and BellSouth jointly own Cingular Wireless ; Verizon has a joint venture with Vodafone Group that offers Verizon wireless service in the U.S .) have expanded their bundled service offerings to include wireless options that neither the cable companies nor the CLECs can so readily offer. There appears to be strong market pressure on these cable companies and CLECs to establish relationships with wireless carriers not affiliated with the ILECs to offer a bundled service that includes wireless service . AT and T is testing a bundled package that includes wireless service from its former wireless unit, AT and T Wireless Services.[40] But there are a limited - and apparently shrinking -number of unaffiliated wireless carriers. Indeed, the announcement on February 17, 2004 that AT and T Wireless has accepted an acquisition bid made by Cingular[41] could remove AT and T Wireless as an independent source of wireless service for AT and T if the acquisition is completed[42]

Similarly, wireless carriers now are offering bundled packages that include local, long distance, and Internet access services, and satellite providers are offering various video packages and experimenting with non-video services . These companies seek bundle components that will reduce churn .

Table 1 presents a sample of bundled service offerings of major providers prepared by one industry observer . It is presented with the caveat that some of the specific bundles, prices, and geographic reaches listed are already out of date because virtually every week some provider is either expanding its bundle, extending the geographic area in which it is offering its bundle, or changing its prices .

Table 1. A Sample of Bundled Service Offerings of Major Providers

Package	Components	Price	A a ability
AT and T DSL Service with One Rate USA	Unlimited local, local toll, and long distance phone service, and DSL	$89.90 to $94.90*	NJ, NY, MD, MA, VA
BellSouthUltimate Answers	Unlimited local, local toll, and long distance phone service, DSL, and 500 Cingular wireless minutes and 5,000 minutes nights and weekends	$124.98 in GA (prices vary in other states)	Nine states in BellSouth territory
Comcast Corp .'s bundle	High-speed Internet, cable TV	$15 discount on Internet :$42.95 down from $57.95**	35 states plus DC
The Cox Value Bundle	Cable TV, unlimited local and long distance phone service with feature package and high-speed Internet	$120.89	New England
MCI's NeighborhoodHiSpeed	limited local, local toll, and long distance phone service, and DSL	$84.99 to $109.99	29 states plus DC
Owest's Simply Phone Service	Unlimited local and domestic long distance and various premium calling features	$49.99 [add unlimited local wireless for $49.99 or add DSL for $29.99]	Most areas of CO, ID, IA, MN, NE, ND, NM, OR, SD, UT, WA, and WY
SBC Total Connections	Unlimited local, local toll, and long distance phone service, DSL, and 300 anytime wireless minutes [Cingular Wireless] and 5,000 minutes nights and weekends	$90 to $95	AK, CA, CT, IL, KS, MI, MO, NV, OH, OK, TX, WI
Sprint Complete Sense Unlimited with PCS	Unlimited local, local toll, and long distance phone service and unlimited wireless	$179.99 to $189.99	36 states plus DC
Verizon Freedom All	Unlimited local, local toll, and long distance phone service, DSL, and 400 anytime wireless minutes, unlimited nights and weekends and 1,000 mobile-to-mobile minutes	$114.89 to $124.89	MA, NJ, NY, PA, VA
Vonage Premium Unlimited Plan	U ed local, local toll, and long s ce phone service	34.99***	50 states

Source: Josh Long, "Unwrapping the Bundle : Telcos Tout Retention Factor, But Packages Reduce Profit Margins," [http://www.xchangemag .com/articles/3clcoverstoryl .htm 1], viewed on 1/6/2004. * excludes $20 discount first three months on DSL; ** excludes the charge for cable television service available at various levels depending on the specific service chosen ; *** excludes charges for a telephone line and DSL service or for cable modem service that are needed in order to use Vonage's service.

THE PRICING OF BUNDLED SERVICE OFFERINGS

The pricing structure of bundled offerings tends to follow a few patterns . Bundled telephone service typically includes unlimited local, local toll, and long distance services at a single flat rate . It sometimes is difficult for consumers to compare that single rate to the sum of the rates of the components because the components (especially long distance and local toll service), when sold as standalone services, usually are sold on a usage (rather than flat rate) basis . Typically, the flat rate bundle is the cheaper option for consumers who are heavy telephone users, but the more expensive choice for consumers who are light users. According to a Wall Street Journal article,[43] "Some people who don't make a lot of calls and don't want services like call waiting soon discover that most unlimited packages, which are geared to high-end customers, aren't economical for them ." This partially explains why MCI's Neighborhood product, "which costs $50 to $60 a month in most areas, loses about half its new customers within the first six months, though turnover drops after that." [44]

ILECs and CLECs that supplement their wireline telephone bundles with non-wireline telephone services, such as high-speed Internet access or wireless service or even video service, typically offer a bundle of their "traditional" services at a fixed price and then allow customers to add to that bundle by paying flat prices for additional services, with the prices for those additional services typically being lower when purchased as part of the bundle than the stand-alone prices for those additional services. Similarly, cable companies typically will supplement their subscription television offerings with high-speed Internet access and telephone services that have a separate add-on price that is lower than the stand-alone price for those services .

According to a New York Times article,[45] "Cable companies, which face little competition from rival cable companies in many markets, have a great deal of leverage in pricing and are eager to expand their universe of high-speed Internet customers because the business has a higher margin than the video business. Cable customers who buy both the video package and high-speed Internet access pay somewhat less than customers who buy only Internet service ." A perhaps more nuanced explanation for this pricing behavior is that cable companies' only competitors for subscription television are the satellite companies, which in most circumstances cannot offer their customers competitive high-speed Internet access service. Cable companies thus can reduce competitive churn by offering high-speed Internet service at a discount that is available only when the customer also takes cable service. For example, cable customers who switch to DirecTV to get their sports package likely will pay $49 for high-speed Internet access from their cable company, but would only have to pay $39 for that service if they bought it along with cable service.[46]

The price for the bundle, or for add-ons to the bundle, sometimes will vary by customer class, with discounts offered only to new customers or only to customers that the provider is trying to "win back" from another provider or only to some other targeted group of customers. For example, the ILECs are making aggressive efforts to woo back customers with extra incentives, including Visa gift cards and special discounts or credits available only to returning customers.[47] Similarly, cable companies are making aggressive efforts to win back subscription video customers from satellite video providers and high-speed Internet access customers from ILECs . As discussed below in the section on Bundling and Competition, sometimes these efforts can lead to claims that the incumbent is engaging in a price war or even predatory or other anticompetitive pricing behavior .

Bundling, while an effective strategy for reducing churn among high-end customers, also will result in previously full-price customers switching to discount plans, according to Jeffrey Halpern of Sanford C . Bernstein and Co.[48] According to a research report prepared by Roger Sachs, of Cathay Financial, sales of bundled packages have had a mixed impact on the balance sheet: "While churn rates have been reduced, [Bell] profit margins are falling under pressure . In an effort to reduce local churn, SBC has aggressively provided high-speed data and long-distance service at the expense of profitability.[49]

Bundling appears to be primarily a strategy for deterring chum among high-usage customers, at the expense of profit margins . One possible consequence of bundling is that providers will feel the need to buttress their overall profit margins by raising the rates for their stand-alone services, which are the services most frequently purchased by low-usage customers . These customers tend to be less price sensitive than larger users and thus tend to be loyal to their traditional providers . Similarly, low-income and elderly customers are less likely than more affluent and younger customers to seek high-speed Internet access and wireless services, and thus more likely to purchase stand-alone telephone services rather than bundled service offerings .

PUBLIC POLICY ISSUES CREATED BY BUNDLING

Bundling potentially creates several public policy issues for Congress, including the on-going viability of the current funding mechanism for the federal Universal Service Fund, proper treatment of taxes that are assessed on only a subset of services included in a bundled offering, and maintaining competitive markets .

Bundling and the Federal Universal Service Fund

Bundled offerings typically include some combination of interstate telecommunications services, international telecommunications services, intrastate telecommunications services, and non-telecommunications services (information services, such as Internet access, video services, and even customer premises equipment) for a single price . The federal Universal Service Fund - the federal subsidy program that assures affordable telephone rates for high-cost (rural) and low-income telephone customers as well as for schools, libraries, and rural health facilities - is supported by an assessment on interstate and international telecommunications revenues only.[50] But it is difficult to identify the portion of revenues generated by a bundled service offering attributable to the interstate and international telecommunications portion of that bundle . Providers must assign a portion of the bundled price to interstate and international telecommunications services and the fund administrators must be able to audit the attribution to protect against companies gaming the system by understating the interstate and international telecommunications portion . There often is no way, however, to unambiguously assign a portion of the revenues to interstate and international telecommunications, and thus there is uncertainty for both providers and administrators .

This is not a trivial problem . With more than 40% of residential customers now purchasing bundled services (and many business customers obtaining complex bundles of services or bandwidth),[51] it is no longer a simple task to identify interstate and international telecommunications revenues . The federal Universal Service assessment on interstate and international revenues for the first quarter of 2004 is 8.7% [52] Providers usually choose to recover this cost directly from their customers, who would prefer to avoid the assessment .

Providers therefore have the incentive to offer their bundled service offerings in a fashion that allows them to minimize the portion of the bundled price attributable to interstate and international telecommunications . Reporting and auditing the interstate and international telecommunications portion of provider revenues is a difficult task .

At the same time, as shown in table 2, the Universal Service assessment base - total interstate and international telecommunications end-user revenues less certain exempt international revenues - has been declining as e-mail and instant messaging increasingly substitute for long distance calling and as long distance rates continue to fall.[53]Although data are not yet available for 2003, it is likely that the assessment base continued to decline in 2003 and continues to decline today as far more customers that are high users of interstate and international service have shifted to bundled service offerings with unlimited usage or high usage levels at flat rates that have continued to fall .

Table 2. Universal Service Assessment Base : Total Interstate and International End-User Revenues Less Certain Exempt Revenues in billions)

Year	Total Interstate and International End-User Revenues Less Certain Exempt Revenues
2002	$76.285
2001	$78.461
2000	$78.977

Source: 2002: Federal-State Joint Board Monitoring Report, released December 2003, table 1 .9, Preliminary 2002 data, at p. 1-32; 2001: Federal-State Joint Board Monitoring Report, released December 2003, table 1 .4, at p. 1-17; 2000: Federal-State Joint Board Monitoring Report, released October 2002, Table 1 .4, at p. 1-16.

As interstate and international telecommunications revenues have begun to fall, and as bundling makes it increasingly difficult to identify and assess those dwindling revenues, many observers are concerned that interstate and international telecommunications revenues no longer provide a sufficient - and sustainable -universal service funding assessment base, as required by the Communications Act.[54] The FCC first issued a Notice of Proposed Rulemaking to address this concern in May 2001,[55] and has subsequently issued additional notices and orders, but to date has taken action only on a few narrow issues. In one action, as mobile wireless telephone service, which typically is offered for a flat rate, has come to be used increasingly for long distance calls, the Commission has increased the "safe harbor" portion of revenues that mobile wireless carriers can attribute to interstate and international calls from 15% to 28 .5%[56] The FCC has been partially constrained in its ability to address the issues relating to bundling and the sufficiency of the Universal Service funding mechanism by the language in the Act and by the Fifth Circuit decision[57]. Some parties have claimed that alternative funding mechanisms would not meet the statutory requirements as interpreted by the court, and that Congressional action would be needed to implement these options.[58]Three options have been proposed to address the issues of bundling and the sufficiency of the Universal Service funding mechanism : expanding the assessment base to include intrastate as well as interstate and international telecommunications services, replacing the current mechanism with a capacity-based assessment on all interstate connections to the public network, and replacing the current mechanism with an assessment on all telephone numbers .

The option to expand the assessment base to include intrastate as well as interstate and international telecommunications services would significantly expand the assessment base,[59] but would only address the reporting and auditing problems created by those bundled service offerings that consist entirely of telecommunications services. It would not address how to attribute the revenues from the interstate, international, and intrastate telecommunications portion of a bundle sold at a flat rate that also includes information services, such as high-speed Internet access, video services, or equipment. Many business customers purchase a fixed amount of bandwidth that they use to provide a wide variety of services - voice, data, Internet access, video conferencing, etc. Currently, many bundled residential offerings that include both telephone service and other services have separate prices for the non-telephone services . But providers will have the incentive to reduce the portion of the bundle subject to the Universal Service assessment on telecommunications services . One way to do this is to simultaneously lower the rate for the telecommunications portion of the bundle and raise the rate for the non-telecommunications portion, but tie the former to the latter so- that customers who do not purchase the non-telecommunications services cannot take advantage of the lower telecom rate . Another way to do this is simply to set a single rate for the bundled telecommunications and non-telecommunications services, with the provider determining the portion to be attributed to telecommunications services and thus subject to assessment. Given the Fifth Circuit decision, a statutory change would be required to allow the FCC to impose a Universal Service assessment on intrastate as well as interstate and international telecommunications revenues .

The option to implement a capacity-based assessment on all interstate connections to the public network would avoid the reporting and auditing problem that currently exists for bundled service offerings because it would be based solely on the capacity of each end-user customer connection to the public network . The FCC, with guidance from Congress, could set assessment rates by weighing various public policy considerations to determine, for example, whether, in order to foster broadband deployment, the assessment on high-speed connections (at least for residential customers) should not be set higher than that on standard voice connections, or whether, for equity reasons, there should be a lower assessment for voice grade connections than for high-speed connections . Also, since all end users ultimately must connect to some network to communicate - no matter what technology they use - the assessment base will be sustained over time . A capacity-based assessment on all connections would be simple to implement and administer for residential customers, but far more difficult for business customers, who use many different connection configurations . Some parties have argued that a connection-based approach would require a statutory change because some interstate carriers do not offer connections and thus such a charge would not meet the statutory requirement that all interstate carriers contribute to the fund on an equitable and nondiscriminatory basis .

The option to implement an assessment on all telephone numbers also would avoid the reporting and auditing problem that currently exists for bundled service offerings because the assessment would be based solely on the number of telephone numbers provided to customers. With each telephone number given the same weight, this approach would treat more intensive and less intensive users of the public network exactly the same . But there are so many telephone numbers that the assessment per telephone number is likely to be relatively small . It is possible that a massive move to Internet protocol technology could result in many parties using "addresses" other than the traditional telephone number, but presumably in that case there would be a way to assess the new address ; some sort of address will always be needed in order to direct communications from a sender to a receiver . Since some interstate telecommunications carriers do not provide telephone numbers, some parties have argued that a statutory change would be required to implement a telephone number-based universal service assessment mechanism, unless a hybrid assessment mechanism were created that assessed on the basis of revenues those providers of interstate services that do not use numbers . Such a hybrid solution might not eliminate the need for a statutory change, however, if the interstate services provided by those carriers are bundled in a fashion that makes it difficult to identify unambiguously the interstate and international revenues generated .

Currently, no bills have been introduced in Congress that directly address the issue of the federal Universal Service assessment base . Both Section 3 of S. 1380, the Rural Universal Service Equity Act of 2003, and Section 4 of H .R. 1582, the Universal Service Fairness Act of 2003, would require the Comptroller General to submit a report to Congress on "the need to reform the high-cost support mechanism for rural, insular, and high cost areas," including a discussion of whether "amendments to section 254 of the Communications Act of 1934 (47 U .S.C. 254) are necessary to preserve and advance universal service." Section 4 of S. 150, the "Internet Tax Non-discrimination Act of 2003, states that "Nothing in the Internet Tax Freedom Act shall prevent the imposition or collection of any fees or charges used to preserve and advance Federal universal service or similar State programs authorized by section 254 of the Communications Act of 1934 ." Bundling and Taxes.

In addition to the federal Universal Service Fund, there are a number of taxes that are assessed on one or more, but not all, of the services included in various bundled service offerings. This creates the same assessment and auditing problem for these taxes as exists for the federal Universal Service Fund .

In particular, many state and local jurisdictions assess taxes on telephone and/or video services. How should those taxes be assessed on bundled services offered at a flat-rate that include telephone service and high-speed Internet access service or cable service and high-speed Internet access service? How can providers identify and report, and state and local tax collectors audit, the taxable portion of such bundles? The Internet Tax Freedom Act moratorium on taxing Internet access (P.L .107-75) has expired. S. 150, S. 52, and H.R. 49 would make the moratorium permanent; H.R . 1481 would extend the moratorium until 2008. Since it is likely that Internet access services increasingly will be bundled with other services that are subject to local or state taxes, if the Internet tax moratorium is extended the challenge of appropriately assessing and auditing these taxes will grow.

Bundling and Competition

Some observers have been concerned that bundled service offerings could have anticompetitive consequences if they foster industry consolidation or if a provider has market power for one of the services in its bundled offering and can use that offering to tie that service to a competitive service in a fashion that reduces competition for the competitive service .

Although it is too early to determine which providers ultimately will benefit most by the trend toward bundled service offerings, the early market results suggest that the ILECs have been more successful at capturing long distance customers than the long distance companies have been at capturing local customers . Despite the fact that the long distance carriers had been able to offer bundles of local and long distance services for months or even years before some of the Regional Bell Operating Companies ("RBOCs") received FCC permission to offer long distance service within their services areas, the RBOCs have captured four long distance customers for every local customer captured by the long distance carriers, as shown in table 3 .

Table 3. "Non-traditional" Customers Captured by Local and Long Distance Carriers

Traditional Local Carrier	Long Distance Customers Captured	Traditional Long Distance Carrier	Local Customers Captured
Verizon	15.9 million	AT and T	3.5 million
SBC	11 .5 million	MCI	3.5 million
BellSouth	3.4 million	Sprint	0.2 million*

Source: Griff Witte, "An Evolutionary Edge: Local Phone Firms Pass Long-Distance Companies," Washington Post, December 3, 2003, at p. El . All data provided by the companies. Numbers for traditionally local companies include a limited number of business customers. *Sprint also has 5.3 million local customers in the various territories where it also is the incumbent local exchange carrier.

According to a J.D. Power and Associates consumer survey, 40% of the respondents stated they would most likely choose their local telephone company to provide bundled services, 21% would most likely choose their long distance company, and 16% their cable company[60]. According to company officials, Verizon now has signed up more than 50% of its local residential customers in some states for long distance service; by contrast, AT and T has signed up at most 15% of its customers to local as well as long distance service.[61] According to Kate Griffin, a senior analyst with the Yankee Group, "The local providers have an edge . The local relationship is worth more . Customers are more likely to look to the local provider for that bundled offering.[62]

It may be too soon to conclude how this competition will play out, however . The RBOCs' success may be explained in part by the fact that for more than 20 years residential customers have been choosing among competitive long distance carriers and thus they are not reluctant to switch to their ILEC when that ILEC begins to offer long distance service. On the other hand, residential customers for the first time can choose their local provider and perhaps many simply are not yet ready to change their behavior.

As explained earlier, bundles appeal primarily to heavy telecommunications users . Heavy long distance users already are used to choosing among - and changing - carriers. Heavy local users, however, are just becoming accustomed to choice in local service. Also, local service provides the "lifeline" to the outside and thus customers may tend to be more cautious about leaving their traditional local provider. This pattern may change as customers become used to having local as well as long distance options . Moreover, as local and long distance telephone services become elements of larger bundled offerings that include wireless, video, high-speed Internet access, and other services, the competitive options available to consumers increasingly will come from non-wireline providers .

If there still are impediments to the competitive provision of one of the services included in a bundled offering, however, bundling could allow those providers that are not constrained by those impediments to extend their market advantage beyond the market for that particular service into the markets for the other services included in the bundled offering. According to a study performed by a coalition of small CLECs,[63] the RBOCs have a 61% share of the customers currently using bundled service offerings that include both local and long distance service, and 80% of the remaining customers for bundles that include local and long distance service are served by the unbundled network element known as the platform ("UNE-P") leased from the RBOCs.[64] Under current conditions, if CLECs were to be denied access to UNE-P to offer local residential service, many would not be able to compete with the RBOCs for the provision of bundled local-long distance service . Given the popularity of such bundled services, this likely would allow the RBOCs to extend their advantage in the local market (by dint of their historical position as the monopoly providers with ubiquitous local networks) into the long distance market . Any harm to consumers from lack of competitive choice might be ameliorated, however, by the extent to which other providers could enter to offer bundled local and long distance service. For example, cable companies or other potential competitors could use voice over Internet protocol (VoIP) to offer competitive bundled local-long distance service . Such service may require a customer to have high-speed Internet access, but the high-usage customers most attracted to bundled services often are the consumers most likely to have high-speed Internet access .

A number of CLECs and CLEC customers have brought antitrust suits against RBOCs, alleging that the RBOCs violated the antitrust laws by not making their unbundled network elements available in a timely and viable fashion.[65] The U.S . Supreme Court, however, ruled on January 13, 2004, in Verizon Communications Inc. v. Law Offices of Curtis V. Trinko, LLP,[66] that failure to meet the unbundling requirements in the 1996 Telecommunications Act, which were intended to foster competition by aiding competitors, does not meet the pre-existing antitrust standards, which relate only to acts that would lessen competition, and thus does not represent an antitrust violation . To the extent that access to UNEs are needed for the competitive provision of bundled service offerings, then, oversight can only be performed by federal and state regulatory agencies, not by the antitrust authorities.

Bundling also could affect the competitive environment if it provides a vehicle for a provider with some market power in the market for one of the bundled service elements to price in a fashion that undermines competition in the market for other services in the bundle. Dominant firms typically are constrained in their ability to practice predatory pricing or other potentially anticompetitive types of strategic pricing against new entrants because it is very difficult to introduce selective price cuts for those customers they want to keep away from competitors without giving the same price discount to a large portion of their customer base. This could so dilute revenues and profits in the short term that such losses could not be recouped in the long term even if competitive entry were retarded or entirely eliminated. To the extent a dominant provider attempting to fend off competitive entry could limit the price cuts to those customers most likely to shift providers and to a limited period of time, the potential for anticompetitive predatory or strategic pricing increases . Bundling might be a tool that could facilitate this.

For example, observers have speculated that cable companies, which are the largest providers of high-speed Internet service, might be able to impede ILEC entry into that market by selectively reducing prices for their cable modem services when ILEC entry is imminent . Such concern was kindled recently when Comcast made a targeted e-mail offer to certain customers in California, Maryland, and Illinois, for cable modem service at $19 .95 per month for a year.[67] After the promotional period, the price goes back to $42 .95. Comcast executive vice president for marketing Dave Watson stated that "This highly targeted e-mail offer is a test campaign aimed directly at DSL customers. It is similar to other win-back-type programs we've conducted in the past. This particular campaign is a limited offer and we anticipate it to be a one-time event as other offers of shorter duration such as 6 months have proven successful." But if Comcast (or any other provider of high-speed Internet access service or any other service that is part of a bundled service offering) has the ability to selectively restrict price cuts to those customers most likely to shift to a competitor and to the time period when a competitor is entering the market, some observers say, then there is at least some potential for that dominant firm to strategically restrict competition in the market even if it is not practicing predatory pricing. The lower prices benefit the selected customers in the short run but can be harmful to the public if they successfully forestall competitive entry . Consumers would then be denied the competition-driven benefits of lower prices and more innovation in the long run .

Another potential competitive consequence of the trend toward bundled service offerings is the incentive created for firms to consolidate in order to more efficiently provide broad bundled offerings or to deny competitors access to independent providers of services needed to offer a complete bundle of services . As explained earlier, consumer preference for larger bundled offerings tends to favor large companies able to offer all or most of the services in the bundle on their own, without reliance on independent entities . But no provider today has the capability of providing all these services. This has fostered marketing agreements and other relationships, which could be a precursor for more formal ownership consolidation . Such consolidation potentially reduces administrative and coordination expenses . But such consolidation also potentially locks up suppliers .

For example, consider the strategy of bundling wireline and wireless service discussed in the section on Wireline, Wireless, and Video Bundling Strategies. The three largest ILECs, Verizon, SBC, and BellSouth, each have large equity interests in wireless carriers, and each have bundled offerings that combine wireless and wireline service . Other wireline carriers face strong market pressure to offer bundles of wireline and wireless services as well. AT and T has a pilot program to offer bundled service in conjunction with AT and T Wireless, which had been part of AT and T but now is independent . AT and T Wireless, however, has announced that it is accepting Cingular's bid to acquire AT and T Wireless . For Cingular, and its parents, SBC and BellSouth, acquisition of AT and T Wireless would provide economies of scale and needed spectrum in large markets such as New York where Cingular has limited spectrum. In addition, such a purchase would take away from AT and T an independent source of wireless service and perhaps make it more difficult for AT and T to offer a bundle that includes wireless service .

CONCLUSION

The bundling of residential telephone, Internet, and video services has been warmly welcomed by consumers. It allows providers to reduce costly customer churn and exploit marketing efficiencies that they have passed through to consumers by lowering rates . But bundling represents a strategic response to the convergence of previously distinct markets and that convergence is creating the need to review current telecommunications law and rules . Leaders in both the House and the Senate Commerce Committees have indicated that review and reform of the 1996 Telecommunications Act will be on the agenda in the 109` Congress . Major issues that are likely to be addressed include creation of a sufficient and sustainable funding mechanism for the federal Universal Service Fund as interstate telecommunications revenues continue to decline (and become increasingly difficult to identify as bundling proliferates), the proper regulatory treatment of services that are provided by different underlying technologies but compete with one another, and the best regulatory framework for fostering innovation and investment while safeguarding consumers and competition. All three of these issues are likely to be affected by the deployment of Voice over Internet Protocol (VoIP) technology, which already has begun to occur .

REFERENCES

[1]   ILECs are the carriers that were the monopoly providers of retail local telephone service before the 1996 Telecommunications Act opened up local markets to competition .

[2]   CLECs are the companies - including the traditional long distance carriers - that began providing local telephone service after the 1996 Act removed statutory prohibitions on competitive provision of local service .

[3]   See "Stevens Foresees Telecom Act II in 2005," Communications Daily, January 27, 2004, at pp 1-2 . ;`Barton Seeking to Lead House Commerce Committee," Communications Daily, February 5, 2004, at pp. 1-2 ; and "Analysts Tell House to Expect Dynamic VOID Growth Soon," Communications Daily, February 5, 2004, at pp. 5-6 .

[4]   See Shawn Young, "Phone-Service Bundles Could Backfire as Customers Switch," Wall Street Journal, November 7, 2003, at p . B-1 .

[5]   J.D. Power and Associates 2003 Residential Long Distance Service Study press release, "Customer Satisfaction Increases as Stiff Rate Competition and Bundling Cause Steep Drop in Long Distance Spending," July 1, 2003, at p. 1, posted on [http://www.jdpower.com/news/releases/index .asp] .

[6]   Griff Witte, "An Evolutionary Edge: Local Phone Firms Pass Long-Distance Companies," Washington Post, December 3, 2003, at p. El, citing Yankee Group senior analyst Kate Griffin .

[7]   Ibid at p. El .

[8]   According to the J .D. Power and Associates 2003 Residential Local Telephone Customer Satisfaction Study press release, "Household Switching of Local Service Carriers Increases as New Players Enter the Local Telephone Service Market," July 15,

2003, at p . 1, posted on [http://www.jdpower.com/news/releases/index.asp], "The number of households reporting they have switched local telephone service carriers in the last year has increased more than 60 percent in 2003, rising to 10 percent from 7 percent in 2002 ." Similarly, according to the J .D. Power and Associates 2003 Residential Cable/Satellite TV Customer Satisfaction Study press release, "Average Monthly Spending for Satellite Service Drops Below Cable Service for the First Time as Cable Market Share Continues to Decline," August 19, 2003, at p. 1, posted on [http://www.jdpower.com/news/releases/index.asp], "Currently, 60 percent of households surveyed subscribe to cable service, down from 68 percent five years ago, while satellite subscriptions have increased from 7 percent of households in 1998 to 17 percent in 2003 ."

[9]   See footnote 12 below .

[10]   Glenn Bischoff, "The Principal of Portability," Wireless Review, November 1, 2003, at p. 11 .

[11]   J.D. Power and Associates 2003 U.S. Wireless Regional CSI Study press release, "Customer Loyalty Becoming a More Critical Issue in the Wireless Industry as Phone Number Portability is Poised to Become a Reality in November," September 30, 2003, at p. 1, posted on [http://www.jdpower.com/news/releases/index.asp] .

[12]   See, for example, Glenn Bischoff, "The Principal of Portability," Wireless Review, November 1, 2003, at p. 11, Tim McElligott, "Churn plus portability equals Y2K-03," Wireless Review, September 1, 2003, at p . 35, and Aude Lagorce, "The Battle Over Cell Phone Business Accounts," Forbes.com, http://www.forbes.com/2003/11/13 /ex-al-1113phones .html ,viewed on January 6, 2004. The J.D. Power and Associates 2003 ..U.S. Wireless Regional CSI Study press release, "Customer Loyalty Becoming a More Critical Issue in the Wireless Industry as Phone Number Portability is Poised to Become a Reality in November," September 30, 2003, at p . 1, posted on http://www.jdpower.com/news/releases/index [.asp], states that 26% of the subscribers in its survey stated they had switched wireless carriers at least once in the past 12 months . Since some of those subscribers may have switched carriers more than once, this suggests a churn rate in excess of 26% .

[13]   According to Richard Wolniewicz, "Building a better business one customer at a time," http://telephonyonline.com/ar/telecom [building_better business/], November 12, 2003, (viewed 1/12/04), "Customer churn is one of the most pressing issues the telecommunications industry faces and it affects all types of carriers from cable operators to mobile service providers . According to a study by Bain and Co ., companies can boost revenues by as much as 85% if they can retain only 5% more of their best customers ."

[14]   High churn-related costs may have been responsible for the ineffectiveness of one of the provisions in the 1996 Telecommunications Act intended to foster competitive entry. Section 252(d)(3) requires the ILECs to make their retail services available to new entrants at wholesale rates determined "on the basis of retail rates charged to subscribers for the telecommunications service requested, excluding the portion thereof attributable to any marketing, billing, collection, and other costs that will be avoided by the local exchange carrier." In implementing this requirement, the FCC adopted a rule instructing states to set wholesale rates by using a methodology that subtracted from retail rates the ILECs' embedded retail-related costs, which were in the range of 15%-

20% of retail rates .This is sometimes called the wholesale "discount" off retail rates . With competitive entry, and the resultant customer churn, however, marketing and sales costs for both entrants and incumbents have risen significantly, and far exceed the 15%-20% discount off retail rates . New entrants therefore have not found it viable to enter the market by reselling retail ILEC services at the discounted wholesale rates . The ILECs, on the other hand, have argued successfully in court that the "discount" off the retail price should be reduced, not increased, because some retail costs are fixed, will not decline in proportion to the number of customers lost to the resellers, and therefore "will not be avoided." (Iowa Utilities II, 8' Federal Circuit Court of Appeals, 219 F3 .d at 754). The 8' Circuit has remanded the FCC's wholesale pricing rule back to the Commission, which has opened up a proceeding to address that and other cost rules .

[15] Among the many firms that collect data and/or perform chum analysis for providers are Convergys' Knowledge Management Services, Yankee Group, In-Stat/MDR, Zelos Group, iGillottResearch Inc ., Gartner Group, Solomon Wolff Associates, Athene Software, Convergence Consulting Group, Compete Inc ., and Dietrich Lockhard Group .

[16] See, for example, Keith Damsell, "Telecom bundling seen luring customers ; Grouping services together for lower price builds loyalty, trims `churn,' study says," The Globe and Mail, 29 September 2003, at p. B8, citing Convergence Consulting Group Ltd . study, The Battle for the North American Couch Potato, and referring to Cox Communications' extremely low churn rate with the "triple play" of digital television, high-speed Internet access, and local telephone service .

[17] See Griff Witte, "An Evolutionary Edge: Local -Phone Firms Pass Long-Distance Companies," Washington Post, December 3, 2003, at p . E1 .

[18] Vince Vittore and Glenn Bischoff, "Bundling Strategy Provides Soft Landing," Telephony, October 7, 2003, at pp . 6-9 .

[19] For example, Covad Communications, which offers high-speed Internet access service using DSL technology, increasingly markets its services through the bundled service offerings of CLECs . See, for example, "AT and T, Covad Extend Consumer Bundle in Midwest States," at [http://www.phoneplusmag.com/hotnews/3chll123256 .htm], viewed 1 on 1/7/2004. Covad's marketing partnerships with many CLECs also have been motivated in part by the FCC's Triennial Review Order, 47 CFR Part 51, "Review of the Section 251 Unbundling Obligations of Incumbent Local Exchange Carriers ; Implementation of the Local Competition Provisions of the Telecommunications Act of 1996 ; Deployment of Wireline Services Offering Advanced Telecommunications Capability; Final Rule and Proposed Rule," Federal Register, Vol .68, No. 169, September 2, 2003, at pp . 52276ff . That Order phases out the "line sharing" requirement, under which companies such as Covad could lease from the ILEC, at cost-based rates, the "data" portion of the local loop to a customer's premises to offer that customer high-speed Internet access service while that customer continued to receive voice service from the ILEC . At the same time, the Order imposed a "line splitting" requirement, under which an ILEC must make the local loop available in such a fashion that a CLEC, such as Covad, that specializes in offering high-speed Internet access (data) service, and another CLEC, such as AT and T or MCI, that specializes in offering voice services, could j ointly use the loop to provide the customer both voice and Internet access services . Under line splitting, one of the CLECs leases the entire loop

from the ILEC at cost-based rates. The two CLECs then work out between themselves the charges for use of the two (voice and data) portions . The ILEC is merely obligated to make it physically possible for the two CLECs to split the loop, for example, by allowing the CLECs to collocate their equipment with one another within the ILEC's central office .

[20] See, for example, Shawn Young, "Phone-Service Bundles Could Backfire as Customers Switch," Wall StreetJournal, November 7, 2003, at p. Bi, quoting Wayne Huyard, president of mass markets for MCI : "Churn has increased. We are entering an era of commoditization for local and long distance ."

[21] UNE-platform consists of the combination of the local loop from the customer premise to the ILEC's central office and the switch port at the central office .

[22] The 1996 Telecommunications Act attempted to foster competitive provision of local telephone service by requiring the ILECs to make available to new entrants those elements of the ILEC networks to which the new entrants needed access in order not to be "impaired" in their ability to offer local service . This requirement that the ILECs unbundlethe elements of their networks and make them available to CLECs should not be confused with the current strategy of many providers to bundleretail services into offerings intended to reduce customer churn .

[23] See "Measuring RBOC Dominance of Bundled-Services : The Progress of Competition Under the New Social Contract," an undated report of the PACE Coalition (a coalition of small CLECs) prepared in late 2003, at p. 3, posted on [www.pacecoalition.com], viewed on 2/10/2004. The FCC's semi-annual report, Local Telephone Competition : Status as of June 30, 2003, which was released in December 2003 and is available at [http://www.fcc.gov/wcb/stats], presents data collected from both ILECs and CLECs for the same period of time . Although it is not possible to directly compare the PACE and FCC data, they appear to describe a consistent scenario. According to the CLEC-provided data presented in table 3 of the FCC report, in June 2003 58 .5% of all CLEC end-user switched access lines were provided using UNEs, 18 .2% were provided by reselling ILEC retail services, and 23.3% were CLEC-owned (i.e .,self-provisioned). According to the CLEC-provided data presented in table 2 of the report, 62% of CLEC end-user switched access lines served residential and small business customers and 38% served large business customers. According to the ILEC-provided data presented in table 4 of the report, 13,026,000 of the 17,231,000 (75 .6%) end-user switched access lines that ILECs have provided to CLECs as UNEs were provided as part of UNE-P (as UNEs with switching) . Virtually none of the access lines self-provisioned by CLECs serve residential or small business customers (the exception being the unusual case of a residential or small business customer being located on the same site as a large business customer) and virtually none of the CLECs' large business customers are served by resold ILEC retail service (ILEC retail service would rarely meet the needs of a large business customer). Also, those CLEC large business customers not served by CLEC-provisioned loops are far more likely than residential and small business customers to have been served by unbundled loops rather than UNE-P, since it is these large business customers that CLECs can serve most efficiently with their own switching. The FCC data suggest that approximately 14 .7% of CLEC switched access lines used UNEs and served large business customers [38% minus 23 .3%] . 44.2% of CLEC switched lines were served by UNE-P [(58.5%)(75.6%)] and 14.3% by UNE-loop [58.5 minus 44.2].

It is likely that virtually all of the 14 .3% of CLEC UNE-loop switched access lines served large business customers, since it is far more efficient to serve these customers than residential and small business customers with UNE-loop . Thus, only about 0.4% of CLEC switched access lines used UNE-platform and served large business customers [14.7% minus 14.3%]. This suggests that 43 .8% of CLEC switched access lines served residential and small business customers using UNE-P, which would be 70% of the 62% of CLEC switched access lines serving residential and small business customers . While this number may be slightly overstated because it implicitly assumes no residential and small business customers are served by UNE-loops, it is not out of line with the 80% PACE findings . The FCC data cover all CLEC lines ; the PACE data cover only those lines sold as part of a bundled local-long distance service offering . While virtually all CLECs that use UNEs are offering such bundles, some of the cable companies, which do not use UNEs, offer local telephone service but not bundled with long distance service. Thus one would expect the figure constructed from the various FCC tables (70%) to be lower than the PACE figure (80%) .

[24] ILECs are not required to offer voice mail because it is an information service, not a telecommunications service, and thus not subject to the 1996 Act's unbundling requirements. Similarly, privacy management services are provided through the ILECs' Advanced Intelligent Networks (AIN), which are proprietary and which the ILECs are not required to make available to CLECs .

[25] To offer its own high-speed Internet service to a customer over ILEC lines, a CLEC must collocate its own DSL equipment (DSLAMs) at a particular point in the ILEC's network . It is only viable to deploy such equipment in places where the CLEC can expect to capture enough customers for the DSL service to justify the investment and where there is space at the ILEC location to place that equipment .

[26] Communications Daily, January 8, 2004, at p. 6 .

[27] In its September 2003 Triennial Review Order, the FCC ended the "line sharing" requirement that ILECs make the data portion of their local loops available to data CLECs at cost-based rates. However, the FCC has grandfathered cost-based prices for the data portion of the customer line for those customers who were served by the high-speed Internet access service provider prior to that Order .

[28] See footnote 19 above .

[29] "SBC Communications Provides Progress Report on Major Growth Strategies, Outlines Broad Service and Cost Initiatives," SBC-Press Room, November 13, 2003, http://www.sbc   [.com/gen/press-room?pid=4800   and   cdvn=news   and newsarticleid=2072 1], viewed on 12/05/2003 . This statement also appears at "SBC Provides 2004 Outlook, Updates Major Trends," [http://convergedigest.com/Bandwidth /sample category article.asp?ID=9406], viewed on 1/9/2004 .

[30] Under the terms of the 1996 Telecommunications Act, the Regional Bell Operating Companies (the old Bell System portions of Verizon, SBC, BellSouth, and Qwest) were required to pass a 14 point checklist demonstrating that their markets have been opened to competitive provision of local telephone service before they were allowed to enter the long haul long distance market in their respective service areas . They have now been approved to offer long distance service in all states .

[31] Griff Witte, "An Evolutionary Edge : Local Phone Firms Pass Long-Distance Companies," Washington Post, December 3, 2003, at p . El .

Bundling Residential Telephone, Internet, and Video Services : Issues for Congress 47

[32] Mike Farrell, "DBS Pitches: MSOs Swine, Telcos Divine," Multichannel News, November 24, 2003, at p . 1, and "BellSouth announces new options," Alexandria Daily Town Talk, December 15, 2003, at p. 8B .

[33] Mike Farrell, "DBS Pitches : MSOs Swine, Telcos Divine," Multichannel News, November 24, 2003, at p. 1 .

[34] National Cable and Telecommunications Association, http://www.ncta[.com/Docs/Page Content.cfm?pageID=9 3], viewed on 1/12/04 .

[35] National Cable and Telecommunications Association, h [ttp://www.ncta.com/Docs/ PageContent .cfm?pageID=32], viewed on 1/12/04 .

[36] See Matt Richtel, "Time Warner Deal Raises Ante in Cable's Bid for Phone Market," New York Times, December 9, 2003 .

[37] According to the J .D. Power and Associates 2003 Residential Cable/Satellite TV Customer Satisfaction Study press release, "Average Monthly Spending for Satellite TV Service Drops Below Cable Service for the First Time as Cable Market Share Continues to Decline," August 19, 2003, at p . 2, posted on [http://www.jdpower.com /news/releases/index .asp], "One area where cable providers may have an opportunity to stem this migration to satellite is in bundling telephony and Internet access with cable TV service . With growing consumer desire to combine multiple services in a single bill for convenience and simplicity, the study finds that 34 percent of cable subscribers want to combine their cable service with some other telecommunications product or service ."

[38] See Matt Stump, "Cable Ops Touting VOD As Anti-Chum Weapon," Broadband Week, March 4, 2003, viewed on [h ttp ://www .broadbandweek .co m /news/020304/020304 cable_cableops.htm] on 1/12/04 .

[39] See Shawn Young, "Phone-Service Bundles Could Backfire as Customers Switch," Wall Street Journal, November 7, 2003, at p. B1 .

[40] Ibid at p. Bl .

[41] "Cingular to Acquire AT and T Wireless, Create Nation's Premier Carrier," February 17, 2004, at [http://www.attwireless .com/press/releases/200 4 releases/021704.ihtml], viewed on 2/17/04 .

[42] Cingular succeeded in an informal auction process created when AT and T Wireless announced in January 2004 that its board of directors had authorized the company to entertain acquisition offers after receiving overtures from nearly half a dozen suitors, including Cingular, Nextel Communications, Vodafone, NIT DoCoMo, and AT and T. See Matt Richtel and Andrew Ross Sorkin, "AT and T Wireless for Sale as a Shakeout Starts,"New York Times, January 21, 2004, at p. Cl. According to the article, the "move by AT and T Wireless and its potential buyers indicates that one of the nation's most fiercely competitive industries is heading toward a long-awaited consolidation that may be the tip of a multilayered and complex merger process around the world."

[43] Shawn Young, "Phone-Service Bundles Could Backfire as Customers Switch," Wall StreetJournal, November 7, 2003, at p . Bl .

[44] Ibid at p. BI. The high chum rates that MCI and other CLECs are experiencing with their bundled services (Adam Quinton, a telecommunications analyst at Merrill Lynch, estimates that turnover in bundled plans offered by rivals to the Bell Operating Companies is as high as 8% a month - or nearly 100% in a year- in some highly competitive areas) also is the result of aggressive ILEC campaigns to "win-back"

customers lost to the CLECs and to the "sticker shock" customers experience because advertised rates typically exclude fees and taxes that can add as much as 15% to the customer bill .

[45] Geraldine Fabrikant, "In Fight Between Cable and Satellite, Customers Gain an Edge," New York Times, December 1, 2003, at p. C22 .

[46] Ibid at p. C22 .

[47] Shawn Young, "Phone-Service Bundles Could Backfire as Customers Switch," "Wall Street Journal, November 7, 2003, at p . BI .

[48] Ibid at p. 131 .

[49] See Josh Long, "Unwrapping the Bundle : Telcos Tout Retention Factor, But Packages Reduce Profit Margins," [http://www.xchangemag.com/articles13clcoverstoryl .htm l], viewed on 1/6/2004 .

[50] The Communications Act, as amended, in Section 254(d) requires "Every telecommunications carrier that provides interstate telecommunications services shall contribute, on an equitable and nondiscriminatory basis, to the specific, predictable, and sufficient mechanisms established by the Commission to preserve and advance universal service." 47 U.S.C. § 254(d) . In Texas Office of Public Utility Counsel v. FCC, 183 F.3d 393 (5 i Cit 0 . 1999), the Fifth Circuit overturned an FCC order assessing intrastate as well as interstate telecommunications to fund the schools and libraries portion of the federal Universal Service Fund, but upheld assessing international telecommunications revenues .

[51] According to the J .D. Power and Associates 2003 Major Provider Business Telecommunications Services Study press release, "More Business Data Customers Willing to Switch Telecommunications Providers in Favor of Cost-Saving Bundles," October 2, 2003, at p. 1, posted on [http://www.jdpower.com/news/releases/index.asp], "The study finds that the intention to switch providers to bundle multiple telecommunications services is up 14 percentage points among broadband business customers to 43 percent overall ."

[52] "Proposed First Quarter 2004 Universal Service Contribution Factor," FCC Public Notice, released December 4, 2003, at p . 1 .

[53] The universal service assessment base is total interstate and international end-user revenues less three exempt categories : revenues for international-to-international service, international revenues where interstate toll represents less than 8% of the company's combined interstate and international revenues, and interstate and international revenues for 2,570 filers who are de minimis and thus not required to contribute . These three categories of exemptions represent approximately 3% of total interstate and international end-user telecommunications revenues .

[54] Section 254(b)(5) of the Communications Act, as amended, lists as a principle that "There should be specific, predictable and sufficient Federal and State mechanisms to preserve and advance universal service." 47 U.S.C. §.

[55] In the Matter of Federal-State Joint Board on Universal Service, Notice of Proposed Rulemaking, CC Docket No. 96-45, released May 8, 2001 .

[56] "In the Matter ofFederal-StateJointBoard on Universal Service, Report and Order and Second Further Notice of Proposed Rulemaking, CC Docket No . 96-45, released December 13, 2002, at p . 14 .

[57] See footnote 50 above .

[58] See, for example, the Comments filed on June 25, 2001 by Verizon and by the United States Telephone Association, responding to the FCC's May 8, 2001 Notice of Proposed Rulemaking inln the Matter ofFederal-StateJointBoard on Universal Service, CC Docket No. 96-45 .

[59] Total End-User Revenues from local service, wireless service, and toll service in 2001, the latest year for which data are available, were $235 .5 billion, $155.3 billion of which were intrastate, according to the FCC's Annual Trends in Telephone Service, table 15.1, "Telecommunications Industry Revenues: 2001," (released inAugust 2003) at p .15-3. This report is available at [www.fcc.gov/wcb/stats] .

[60] J.D. Power and Associates 2003 Residential Long Distance Service Study press release, "Customer Satisfaction Increases as Stiff Rate Competition and Bundling Cause Steep Drop in Long Distance Spending," July 1, 2003, at pp. 1-2, posted on [http://www.jdpower .com/news/releases/index.asp] .

[61] Griff Witte, "An Evolutionary Edge : Local Phone Fi s Pass Long-Distance Companies," Washington Post, December 3, 2003, at p . El .

[62] Ibid at p . El .

[63] "Measuring RBOC Dominance of Bundled-Services: The Progress of Competition Under the New Social Contract," an undated report of the PACE Coalition (a coalition of small CLECs) prepared in late 2003, at p. 3, posted on [www.pacecoalition.com], viewed on 2/10/2004 .

[64] The PACE report claims that only 1% of these customers are served by wireless providers. This suggests that the PACE Coalition only included those wireless customers who have abandoned wireline service entirely and use wireless service as their exclusive provider of local and long distance service .

[65] For example, Trinko and Cavalier brought cases against Verizon, Covad brought a case against BellSouth, and Metronet brought a case against Qwest .

[66] Verizon Communications Inc ., Petitioner v. Law Offices of Curtis V. Trinko, LLP, Supreme Court of the United States, 540 U .S. (2004), January 13, 2004, Slip opinion at 6-7 (2004 WL 51011). For a more complete discussion of the Trinko decision, see CRS Report RS21723, Verizon Communications, Inc . v. Trinko: Telecommunications Consumers Cannot Use Antitrust Laws to Remedy Access Violations of Telecommunications Act .

[67] Communications Daily, November 17, 2003, at p . 7 .

In: Broadband Internet: Access, Regulation and Policy   ISBN: 978-1-60456-073-2
Editor: Ellen S. Cohen, pp. 51-75   © 2007 Nova Science Publishers, Inc.

Chapter 3

BROADBAND INTERNET ACCESS AND THE DIGITAL DIVIDE: FEDERAL ASSISTANCE PROGRAMS[*]

Lennard G. Kruger[1] and Angele A. Gilroy[2]
[1] Science and Technology Resources, Science, and Industry Division
[2] Telecommunications Resources, Science, and Industry Division

ABSTRACT

The "digital divide" is a term that has been used to characterize a gap between "information haves and have-nots," or in other words, between those Americans who use or have access to telecommunications technologies (e.g., telephones, computers, the Internet) and those who do not. One important subset of the digital divide debate concerns high-speed Internet access, also known as *broadband*. Broadband is provided by a series of technologies (e.g. cable, telephone wire, fiber, satellite, wireless) that give users the ability to send and receive data at volumes and speeds far greater than current "dial-up" Internet access over traditional telephone lines.

Broadband technologies are currently being deployed primarily by the private sector throughout the United States. While the numbers of new broadband subscribers continue to grow, studies conducted by the Federal Communications Commission (FCC), the Department of Commerce (DOC), and the Department of Agriculture (USDA) suggest that the rate of broadband deployment in urban and high income areas may be outpacing deployment in rural and low-income areas.

Some policymakers, believing that disparities in broadband access across American society could have adverse economic and social consequences on those left behind, assert that the federal government should play a more active role to avoid a "digital divide" in broadband access. One approach is for the federal government to provide financial assistance to support broadband deployment in underserved areas. Others, however, believe that federal assistance for broadband deployment is not appropriate. Some opponents question the reality of the "digital divide," and argue that federal intervention in the broadband marketplace would be premature and, in some cases, counterproductive.

Legislation introduced (but not enacted) in the 109th Congress sought to provide federal financial assistance for broadband deployment in the form of grants, loans,

---

[*] Excerpted from CRS Report RL30719, dated February 7, 2007.

subsidies, and tax credits. Many of these legislative proposals are likely to be reintroduced into the 110th Congress. Of particular note is the possible reauthorization of the Rural Utilities Service (RUS) broadband program, which is expected to be considered as part of the 2007 farm bill. Legislation to reform universal service – which could have a significant impact on the amount of financial assistance available for broadband deployment in rural and underserved areas – has been introduced into the 110th Congress (H.R. 42, S. 101).

In assessing such legislation, several policy issues arise. For example, is the current status of broadband deployment data an adequate basis on which to base policy decisions? Is federal assistance premature, or do the risks of delaying assistance to underserved areas outweigh the benefits of avoiding federal intervention in the marketplace? And finally, if one assumes that governmental action is necessary to spur broadband deployment in underserved areas, which specific approaches, either separately or in combination, are likely to be most effective?

This report will be updated as events warrant.

BACKGROUND

The "digital divide" is a term used to describe a perceived gap between perceived "information haves and have-nots," or in other words, between those Americans who use or have access to telecommunications technologies (e.g., telephones, computers, the Internet) and those who do not.[1] Whether or not individuals or communities fall into the "information haves" category depends on a number of factors, ranging from the presence of computers in the home, to training and education, to the availability of affordable Internet access. A series of reports issued by the Department of Commerce[2] (DOC) during the Clinton Administration argued that a "digital divide" exists, with many rural citizens, certain minority groups, and low-income Americans tending to have less access to telecommunications technology than other Americans.[3]

In February 2002, the Bush Administration's Department of Commerce released its first survey report on Internet use, entitled *A Nation Online: How Americans Are Expanding Their Use of the Internet*.[4] While acknowledging a disparity in usage between "information haves and have nots," the report focused on the increasing rates of Internet usage among traditionally underserved groups:

> In every income bracket, at every level of education, in every age group, for people of every race and among people of Hispanic origin, among both men and women, many more people use computers and the Internet now than did so in the recent past. Some people are still more likely to be Internet users than others. Individuals living in low-income households or having little education, still trail the national average. However, broad measures of Internet use in the United States suggest that over time Internet use has become more equitable.[5]

A Nation Online: Entering the Broadband Age, published in September 2004, is the sixth Department of Commerce report examining the use of computers, the Internet, and other information technology. For the first time, the DOC report focuses on broadband, also known as high-speed Internet access. Broadband is provided by a series of technologies (e.g. cable, telephone wire, satellite, wireless) that give users the ability to send and receive data at volumes and speeds far greater than current "dial-up" Internet access over traditional telephone lines.[6] The DOC report found that the proportion of U.S. households with broadband connections grew from 9.1% in September 2001 to 19.9% in October 2003.[7]

According to the latest FCC data on the deployment of high-speed Internet connections (released January 2007), as of June 30, 2006 there were 64.6 million high speed lines connecting homes and businesses to the Internet in the United States, a growth rate of 26% during the first half of 2006. Of the 64.6 million high speed lines reported by the FCC, 50.3 million serve residential users.[8] While the broadband *adoption* rate stands at 28% of U.S. households[9], broadband *availability* is much higher. As of June 30, 2006, the FCC found at least one high-speed subscriber in 99% of all zip codes in the United States. The FCC estimates that "roughly 20 percent of consumers with access to advanced telecommunications capability do subscribe to such services." According to the FCC, possible reasons for the gap between broadband availability and subscribership include the lack of computers in some homes, price of broadband service, lack of content, and the availability of broadband at work.[10]

Broadband in Rural and Underserved Areas[11]

While the number of new broadband subscribers continues to grow, the rate of broadband deployment in urban and high income areas appears to be outpacing deployment in rural and low-income areas. In response to a request by ten Senators, the Departments of Commerce and Agriculture released a report on April 26, 2000, concluding that rural areas lag behind urban areas in access to broadband technology. The report found that less than 5% of towns of 10,000 or less have access to broadband, while broadband over cable has been deployed in more than 65% of all cities with populations over 250,000, and broadband over the telephone network has been deployed in 56% of all cities with populations over 100,000.[12]

Similarly, the February 2002 report from the Department of Commerce, *A Nation Online: How Americans Are Expanding Their Use of the Internet*, found that 12.2% of Internet users in rural areas had high-speed connections, as opposed to 21.2% of Internet users in urban areas. The report's survey also found, not surprisingly, that individuals in high-income households have higher broadband subscribership rates than individuals in lower income households.[13]

December 2005 data from the Pew Internet and American Life Project indicate that while broadband adoption is growing in urban, suburban, and rural areas, broadband users make up larger percentages of urban and suburban users than rural users. Pew found that the percentage of all U.S. adults with broadband at home is 38% for urban areas, 40% for suburban areas, and 24% for rural areas.[14]

Similarly, a May 2006 report released by the Government Accountability Office (GAO) found that 17% of rural households subscribe to broadband, as opposed to 28% of suburban and 29% of urban households.[15]

According to the latest FCC data on the deployment of high-speed Internet connections (released January 2007), high-speed subscribers were reported in 99% of the most densely populated zip codes, as opposed to 89% of zip codes with the lowest population densities. Similarly, for zip codes ranked by median family income, high-speed subscribers were reported present in 99% of the top one-tenth of zip codes, as compared to 91% of the bottom one-tenth of zip codes.[16]

On the other hand, the FCC's *Fourth Report*, while acknowledging that disparities in broadband deployment exist, asserts that the gap between the broadband "haves and have-nots" is narrowing:

> [T]he *Fourth Report* also documents the continuation of a positive trend that first emerged in our last report: namely, the increasing availability of advanced telecommunications capability to certain groups of consumers — those in rural areas, those with low incomes, and those with disabilities — who stand in particular need of advanced services. Consumers in these groups are of special concern to the Commission in that they are most in need of access to advanced telecommunications capability to overcome economic, educational, and other limitations, they are also the most likely to lack access precisely *because* of these limitations. The *Fourth Report* demonstrates that we are making substantial progress in closing the gaps in access that these groups traditionally have experienced.[17]

The September 2004 Department of Commerce report, *A Nation Online: Entering the Broadband Age*, found that a lower percentage of Internet households have broadband in rural areas (24.7%) than in urban areas (40.4%), and that "while broadband usage has grown significantly in all areas since the previous survey, the rural-urban differential continues."[18] The report also found that broadband penetration rates are higher in the West and Northeast than in the South and Midwest.[19] Race and ethnicity were also found to be significant determinants of broadband use, with 25.7% of White Americans living in broadband households, as opposed to 14.2% of Black and 12.6% of Hispanic Americans.[20]

Some policymakers believe that disparities in broadband access across American society could have adverse consequences on those left behind. While a minority of American homes today subscribe to broadband, many believe that advanced Internet applications of the future — voice over the Internet protocol (VoIP) or high quality video, for example — and the resulting ability for businesses and consumers to engage in e-commerce, may increasingly depend on high speed broadband connections to the Internet. Thus, some say, communities and individuals without access to broadband could be at risk to the extent that e-commerce becomes a critical factor in determining future economic development and prosperity. A 2003 study conducted by Criterion Economics found that ubiquitous adoption of current generation broadband technologies would result in a cumulative increase in gross domestic product of $179.7 billion, while sustaining an additional 61,000 jobs per year over the next nineteen years. The study projected that 1.2 million jobs could be created if next generation broadband technology is rapidly and ubiquitously deployed.[21] A February 2006 study done by the Massachusetts Institute of Technology for the Economic Development Administration/Department of Commerce marked the first attempt to quantitatively measure the impact of broadband on economic growth. The study found that "between 1998 and 2002, communities in which mass-market broadband was available by December 1999 experienced more rapid growth in employment, the number of businesses overall, and businesses in IT-intensive sectors, relative to comparable communities without broadband at that time."[22]

Some also argue that broadband is an important contributor to U.S. future economic strength with respect to the rest of the world. According to the International Telecommunications Union, the U.S. ranks 16th worldwide in broadband penetration (subscriptions per 100 inhabitants as of December 2005).[23] Similarly, data from the Organization for Economic Cooperation and Development (OECD) found the U.S. ranking 12th among OECD nations in broadband access per 100 inhabitants as of June 2006.[24] By contrast, in 2001 an OECD study found the U.S. ranking 4th in broadband subscribership per 100 inhabitants (after Korea, Sweden, and Canada).[25]

Federal Role

The Telecommunications Act of 1996 (P.L. 104-104) addresses the issue of whether the federal government should intervene to prevent a "digital divide" in broadband access. Section 706 requires the FCC to determine whether "advanced telecommunications capability [i.e., broadband or high-speed access] is being deployed to all Americans in a reasonable and timely fashion." If this is not the case, the act directs the FCC to "take immediate action to accelerate deployment of such capability by removing barriers to infrastructure investment and by promoting competition in the telecommunications market."

On January 28, 1999, the FCC adopted its first report (FCC 99-5) pursuant to Section 706. The report concluded that "the consumer broadband market is in the early stages of development, and that, while it is too early to reach definitive conclusions, aggregate data suggests that broadband is being deployed in a reasonable and timely fashion."[26] The FCC announced that it would continue to monitor closely the deployment of broadband capability in annual reports and that, where necessary, it would "not hesitate to reduce barriers to competition and infrastructure investment to ensure that market conditions are conducive to investment, innovation, and meeting the needs of all consumers."

The FCC's second Section 706 report was adopted on August 3, 2000. Based on more extensive data than the first report, the FCC similarly concluded that notwithstanding risks faced by some vulnerable populations, broadband is being deployed in a reasonable and timely fashion overall:

> Recognizing that the development of advanced services infrastructure remains in its early stages, we conclude that, overall, deployment of advanced telecommunications capability is proceeding in a reasonable and timely fashion. Specifically, competition is emerging, rapid build-out of necessary infrastructure continues, and extensive investment is pouring into this segment of the economy.[27]

The FCC's third Section 706 report was adopted on February 6, 2002. Again, the FCC concluded that "the deployment of advanced telecommunications capability to all Americans is reasonable and timely."[28] The FCC added:

> We are encouraged by the expansion of advanced services to many regions of the nation, and growing number of subscribers. We also conclude that investment in infrastructure for most advanced services markets remains strong, even though the pace of investment trends has generally slowed. This may be due in part to the general economic slowdown in the nation. In addition, we find that emerging technologies continue to stimulate competition and create new alternatives and choices for consumers.[29]

On September 9, 2004, the FCC adopted and released its *Fourth Report* pursuant to Section 706. Like the previous three reports, the FCC concludes that "the overall goal of section 706 is being met, and that advanced telecommunications capability is indeed being deployed on a reasonable and timely basis to all Americans."[30] The FCC notes the emergence of new services such as VoIP, and the significant development of new broadband access technologies such as unlicensed wireless (WiFi)and broadband over power lines. The FCC notes the future promise of emerging multiple advanced broadband networks which can complement one another:

> For example, in urban and suburban areas, wireless broadband services may "fill in the gaps" in wireline broadband coverage, while wireless and satellite services may bring high-speed broadband to remote areas where wireline deployment may be costly. Having multiple advanced networks will also promote competition in price, features, and quality-of-service among broadband-access providers.[31]

Two FCC Commissioners (Michael Copps and Jonathan Adelstein) dissented from the *Fourth Report* conclusion that broadband deployment is reasonable and timely. They argued that the relatively poor world ranking of United States broadband penetration indicates that deployment is insufficient, that the FCC's continuing definition of broadband as 200 kilobits per second is outdated and is not comparable to the much higher speeds available to consumers in other countries, and that the use of zip code data (measuring the presence of at least one broadband subscriber within a zip code area) does not sufficiently characterize the availability of broadband across geographic areas.[32]

While the FCC is currently implementing or actively considering some regulatory activities related to broadband,[33] no major regulatory intervention pursuant to Section 706 of the Telecommunications Act of 1996 has been deemed necessary by the FCC at this time.

Meanwhile, the National Telecommunications and Information Administration (NTIA) at the Department of Commerce (DOC) was tasked with developing the Bush Administration's broadband policy.[34] Statements from Administration officials indicated that much of the policy would focus on removing regulatory roadblocks to investment in broadband deployment.[35] On June 13, 2002, in a speech at the 21st Century High Tech Forum, President Bush declared that the nation must be aggressive about the expansion of broadband, and cited ongoing activities at the FCC as important in eliminating hurdles and barriers to get broadband implemented. President Bush made similar remarks citing the economic importance of broadband deployment at the August 13, 2002 economic forum in Waco, Texas.

Subsequently, a more formal Administration broadband policy was unveiled in March and April of 2004. On March 26, 2004, President Bush endorsed the goal of universal broadband access by 2007. Then on April 26, 2004, President Bush announced a broadband initiative which includes promoting legislation which would permanently prohibit all broadband taxes, making spectrum available for wireless broadband and creating technical standards for broadband over power lines, and simplifying rights-of-way processes on federal lands for broadband providers.[36]

The Bush Administration has also emphasized the importance of encouraging demand for broadband services. On September 23, 2002, the DOC's Office of Technology Policy released a report, *Understanding Broadband Demand: A Review of Critical Issues*,[37] which argues that national governments can accelerate broadband demand by taking a number of steps, including protecting intellectual property, supporting business investment, developing e-government applications, promoting efficient radio spectrum management, and others. Similarly, the President's Council of Advisers on Science and Technology (PCAST) was tasked with studying "demand-side" broadband issues and suggesting policies to stimulate broadband deployment and economic recovery. The PCAST report, *Building Out Broadband*, released in December 2002, concludes that while government should not intervene in the telecommunications marketplace, it should apply existing policies and work with the private sector to promote broadband applications and usage. Specific initiatives include increasing e-government broadband applications (including homeland security); promoting telework, distance learning, and telemedicine; pursuing broadband-friendly spectrum policies, and ensuring access to public rights of way for broadband infrastructure.[38] Meanwhile, "high-tech" organizations such as TechNet,[39] the Computer Systems Policy Project (CSPP)[40], and the Semiconductor Industry Association (SIA)[41] have called on the federal government to adopt policies toward a goal of 100 Mbs to 100 million homes by the end of the decade.

Some policymakers in Congress assert that the federal government should play a more active role to avoid a "digital divide" in broadband access, and that legislation is necessary to ensure fair competition and timely broadband deployment. Bills were been introduced into the 109th Congress which seek to provide federal financial assistance for broadband deployment in the form of grants, loans, subsidies, and/or tax credits. Similar bills are expected in the 110th Congress.

State and Local Broadband Activities

In addition to federal support for broadband deployment, there are programs and activities ongoing at the state and local level. Surveys, assessments, and reports from the American Electronics Association,[42] Technet,[43] the Alliance for Public Technology,[44] the California Public Utilities Commission,[45] and the AEI-Brookings Joint Center[46] have explored state and local broadband programs. A related issue is the emergence of municipal broadband networks (primarily wireless and fiber based) and the debate over whether such networks constitute unfair competition with the private sector (for more information on municipal broadband, see CRS Report RS20993, *Wireless Technology and Spectrum Demand: Advanced Wireless Services*, by Linda K. Moore).

FEDERAL TELECOMMUNICATIONS DEVELOPMENT PROGRAMS

Table 1 (at the end of this report) shows selected federal domestic assistance programs throughout the federal government that can be associated with telecommunications development. Many (if not most) of these programs can be related, if not necessarily to the deployment of broadband technologies in particular, then to telecommunications and the "digital divide" issue generally.

The Universal Service Concept and the FCC[47]

Since its creation in 1934 the Federal Communications Commission (FCC) has been tasked with "... mak[ing] available, so far as possible, to all the people of the United States, ... a rapid, efficient, Nation-wide, and world-wide wire and radio communications service with adequate facilities at reasonable charges...."[48] This mandate led to the development of what has come to be known as the universal service concept.

The universal service concept, as originally designed, called for the establishment of policies to ensure that telecommunications services are available to all Americans, including those in rural, insular and high cost areas, by ensuring that rates remain affordable. Over the years this concept fostered the development of various FCC policies and programs to meet this goal. The FCC offers universal service support through a number of direct mechanisms that target both providers of and subscribers to telecommunications services.[49]

The development of the federal universal service high cost fund is an example of provider-targeted support. Under the high cost fund, eligible telecommunications carriers, usually those serving rural, insular and high cost areas, are able to obtain funds to help offset the higher than average costs of providing telephone service.[50] This mechanism has been particularly important to rural America where the lack of subscriber density leads to significant costs. FCC universal service policies have also been expanded to target individual users. Such federal programs include two income-based programs, Link Up and Lifeline, established in the mid-1980s to assist economically needy individuals. The Link Up program assists low-income subscribers pay the costs associated with the initiation of telephone service and the Lifeline program assists low-income subscribers pay the recurring monthly service charges. Funding to assist carriers providing service to individuals with speech and/or hearing disabilities is also provided through the Telecommunications Relay Service Fund. Effective January 1, 1998, schools, libraries, and rural health care providers also qualified for universal service support.

Universal Service and the Telecommunications Act of 1996

Passage of the Telecommunications Act of 1996 (P.L.104-104) codified the long-standing commitment by U.S. policymakers to ensure universal service in the provision of telecommunications services.

The Schools and Libraries, and Rural Health Care Programs

Congress, through the 1996 Act, not only codified, but also expanded the concept of universal service to include, among other principles, that elementary and secondary schools and classrooms, libraries, and rural health care providers have access to telecommunications services for specific purposes at discounted rates. (See Sections 254(b)(6) and 254(h)of the 1996 Telecommunications Act, 47 USC 254.)

1. The Schools and Libraries Program. Under universal service provisions contained in the 1996 Act, elementary and secondary schools and classrooms and libraries are designated as beneficiaries of universal service discounts. Universal service principles detailed in Section 254(b)(6) state that "Elementary and secondary schools and classrooms ... and libraries should have access to advanced telecommunications services..." The act further requires in Section 254(h)(1)(B) that services within the definition of universal service be provided to

elementary and secondary schools and libraries for education purposes at discounts, that is at "rates less than the amounts charged for similar services to other parties."

The FCC established the Schools and Libraries Division within the Universal Service Administrative Company (USAC) to administer the schools and libraries or "E (education)-rate" program to comply with these provisions. Under this program, eligible schools and libraries receive discounts ranging from 20 to 90 percent for telecommunications services depending on the poverty level of the school's (or school district's) population and its location in a high cost telecommunications area. Three categories of services are eligible for discounts: internal connections (e.g. wiring, routers and servers); Internet access; and telecommunications and dedicated services, with the third category receiving funding priority. According to data released by program administrators, $17 billion in funding has been committed over the first eight years of the program with funding released to all states, the District of Columbia and all territories. Funding commitments for funding Year 2006 (July 1, 2006 - June 30, 2007), the ninth and current year of the program, totaled $1.6 billion as of December 5, 2006.[51]

2. The Rural Health Care Program. Section 254(h) of the 1996 Act requires that public and non-profit rural health care providers have access to telecommunications services necessary for the provision of health care services at rates comparable to those paid for similar services in urban areas. Subsection 254(h)(1) further specifies that "to the extent technically feasible and economically reasonable" health care providers should have access to advanced telecommunications and information services. The FCC established the Rural Health Care Division (RHCD) within the USAC to administer the universal support program to comply with these provisions. Under FCC established rules only public or nonprofit health care providers are eligible to receive funding. Eligible health care providers, with the exception of those requesting only access to the Internet, must also be located in a rural area.[52] The funding ceiling, or cap, for this support was established at $400 million annually. The funding level for Year One of the program (January 1998 - June 30, 1999) was set at $100 million. Due to less than anticipated demand, the FCC established a $12 million funding level for the second year (July 1, 1999 to June 30, 2000) of the program but has since returned to a $400 million yearly cap. As of December 8, 2006, covering the first nine years of the program, a total of $174.8 million has been committed to 3,440 rural health care providers. The primary use of the funding is to provide reduced rates for telecommunications and information services necessary for the provision of health care.[53]

The Telecommunications Development Fund

Section 714 of the 1996 Act created the Telecommunications Development Fund (TDF). The TDF is a private, non-governmental, venture capital corporation overseen by a seven-member board of directors and fund management. The purpose of the TDF is threefold: to promote access to capital for small businesses in order to enhance competition in the telecommunications industry; to stimulate new technology development and promote employment and training; and to support universal service and enhance the delivery of telecommunications services to rural and underserved areas. The TDF is authorized to provide financing to eligible small businesses in the telecommunications industry through loans and investment capital. At this time the TDF is focusing on providing financing in the form of equity investments ranging from $375,000 to $1 million per investment.[54] Initial funding for the program is derived from the interest earned from the upfront payments bidders submit to participate in FCC auctions. The availability of funds for future investments is dependent on earning a successful return on the Fund's portfolio. As of September 2005, the TDF had $50 million under management of which $16.8million is committed to seventeen portfolio companies.[55]

Universal Service and Broadband

One of the policy debates surrounding universal service is whether access to advanced telecommunications services (i.e. broadband) should be incorporated into universal service objectives. The term universal service, when applied to telecommunications, refers to the ability to make available a basket of telecommunications services to the public, across the nation, at a reasonable price. As directed in the 1996 Telecommunications Act [Section 254(c)] a federal-state Joint Board was tasked with defining the services which should be included in the basket of services to be eligible for federal universal service support; in effect using and defining the term "universal service" for the first time. The Joint Board's recommendation, which was subsequently adopted by the FCC in May 1997, included the following in its universal services package: voice grade access to and some usage of the public switched network; single line service; dual tone signaling; access to directory assistance; emergency service such as 911; operator services; access and interexchange (long distance) service.

Some policy makers expressed concern that the FCC-adopted definition is too limited and does not take into consideration the importance and growing acceptance of advanced services such as broadband and Internet access. They point to a number of provisions contained in the Universal Service section of the 1996 Act to support their claim. Universal service principles contained in Section 254(b)(2) state that "Access to advanced telecommunications services should be provided to all regions of the Nation." The subsequent principle (b)(3) calls for consumers in all regions of the Nation including "low-income" and those in "rural, insular, and high cost areas" to have access to telecommunications and information services including "advanced services" at a comparable level and a comparable rate charged for similar services in urban areas. Such provisions, they state, dictate that the FCC expand its universal service definition.

Others caution that a more modest approach is appropriate given the "universal mandate" associated with this definition and the uncertainty and costs associated with mandating nationwide deployment of such advanced services as a universal service policy goal. Furthermore they state the 1996 Act does take into consideration the changing nature of the telecommunications sector and allows for the universal service definition to be modified if future conditions warrant. Section 254(c)of the act states that "universal service is an evolving level of telecommunications services" and the FCC is tasked with "periodically" reevaluating this definition "taking into account advances in telecommunications and information technologies and services." Furthermore, the Joint Board is given specific authority to recommend "from time to time" to the FCC modification in the definition of the services to be included for federal universal service support. The Joint Board, in July 2002, concluded such an inquiry and recommended that at this time no changes be made in the current list of services eligible for universal service support. The FCC, in a July 10, 2003 order (FCC 03-170) adopted the Joint Board's recommendation thereby leaving unchanged the list of services supported by Federal universal service.

Rural Utilities Service

The Rural Electrification Administration (REA), subsequently renamed the Rural Utilities Service (RUS), was established by the Roosevelt Administration in 1935. Initially, it was established to provide credit assistance for the development of rural electric systems. In 1949, the mission of REA was expanded to include rural telephone providers. Congress further amended the Rural Electrification Act in 1971 to establish within REA a Rural Telephone Account and the Rural Telephone Bank (RTB). Rural Telephone Loans and Loan Guarantees provide long-term direct and guaranteed loans for telephone lines, facilities, or systems to furnish and improve telecommunications service in rural areas. The RTB – liquidated in FY2006 – was a public-private partnership intended to provide additional sources of capital that would supplement loans made directly by RUS. Another program, the Distance Learning and Telemedicine Program, specifically addresses health care and education needs of rural America.

RUS implements two programs specifically targeted at providing assistance for broadband deployment in rural areas: the Rural Broadband Access Loan and Loan Guarantee Program and Community Connect Broadband Grants. The current authorization for the Rural Broadband Access Loan and Loan Guarantee Program expires on September 30, 2007. It is expected that the 110th Congress will consider reauthorization of the program as part of the 2007 farm bill. For further information on rural broadband and the RUS broadband programs, see CRS Report RL33816, *Broadband Loan and Grant Programs in the USDA's Rural Utilities Service, by* Lennard G. Kruger.

LEGISLATION IN THE 109TH CONGRESS

In the 109th Congress, legislation was introduced to provide financial assistance to encourage broadband deployment (including loans, grants, and tax incentives), and to allocate additional spectrum for use by wireless broadband applications. Of particular note is enactment of the Deficit Reduction Act of 2005 (P.L. 109-171), which set a hard deadline for the digital television transition, thereby reclaiming analog television spectrum to be auctioned for commercial applications such as wireless broadband. A complete listing of bills is provided below.

H.R. 3 (Young, Don)/P.L. 109-59
Transportation Equity Act: A Legacy for Users. Directs the Secretary of Transportation to conduct a study on the feasibility of installing fiber optic cabling and wireless communications infrastructure along rural interstate highway corridors; such study will identify rural broadband access points. Introduced February 9, 2005; referred to Committee on Transportation and Infrastructure. Passed House on March 10, 2005. Passed Senate on May 17, 2005. Signed into law by President on August 10, 2005.

H.R. 144 (McHugh)
Rural America Digital Accessibility Act. Provides for grants, loans, research, and tax credits to promote broadband deployment in underserved rural areas. Introduced January 4,

2005; referred to Committee on Energy and Commerce and the Committee on Ways and Means.

H.R. 146 (McHugh)

Establishes a grant program to support broadband-based economic development efforts. Introduced January 4, 2005; referred to Committee on Transportation and Infrastructure and to Committee on Financial Services.

H.R. 1479 (Udall)

Rural Access to Broadband Service Act. Establishes a Rural Broadband Office within the Department of Commerce which would coordinate federal government resources with respect to expansion of broadband services in rural areas. Directs the National Science Foundation to conduct research in enhancing rural broadband. Expresses the Sense of Congress that the broadband loan program in the Rural Utilities Service should be fully funded. Provides for the expensing of broadband Internet access expenditures for rural communities. Introduced April 5, 2005; referred to Committees on Science and on Energy and Commerce.

H.R. 3517 (Andrews)

Greater Access to E-Governance Act (GATE Act). Establishes a grant program in the Department of Commerce to provide funds to State and local governments to enable them to deploy broadband computer networks for the conduct of electronic governance transactions by citizens in local schools and libraries. Introduced July 28, 2005; referred to Committee on Energy and Commerce.

H.R. 3958 (Melancon)

Louisiana Katrina Reconstruction Act. Provides grants for construction of broadband infrastructure necessary for technology and economic development in areas affected by Hurricane Katrina. Introduced September 29, 2005; referred to multiple committees.

H.R. 5072 (Terry)

Universal Reform Act of 2006. Targets universal service support specifically to eligible telecommunications carriers in high-cost geographic areas to ensure that communications services and high-speed broadband services are made available throughout all of the States of the United States in a fair and equitable manner. Introduced March 30, 2006; referred to Committee on Energy and Commerce.

H.R. 5252 (Barton)

Communications, Opportunity, Promotion, and Enhancement Act of 2006. Establishes Broadband for Unserved Areas Program funded by universal service funding not to exceed $500 million per year (Title II). Prevents states from prohibiting municipal broadband (Title V). Directs FCC to make available eligible broadcast television frequencies ("white space") for unlicensed use (which could include wireless broadband applications) in a manner that protects broadcasters from interference (Title VI). Directs the FCC to periodically revise its definition of broadband above 200 kbps (Title IX). Requires the FCC to collect more detailed broadband deployment data (Title X). Introduced May 1, 2006. Passed House June 8, 2006.

Reported by Senate Committee on Commerce, Science and Transportation with an amendment in the nature of a substitute, September 29, 2006 (S.Rept. 109-355).

H.R. 5970 (Thomas, William)

Estate Tax and Extension of Tax Relief Act of 2006. Provides a tax credit to holders of rural renaissance bonds funding qualified projects including expanding broadband technology in rural areas. Passed House July 29, 2006.

S. 14 (Stabenow)

Fair Wage, Competition, and Investment Act of 2005. Allows the expensing of broadband Internet access expenditures. Introduced January 24, 2005; referred to Committee on Finance.

S. 497 (Salazar)

Broadband Rural Revitalization Act of 2005. Establishes a Rural Broadband Office within the Department of Commerce which would coordinate federal government resources with respect to expansion of broadband services in rural areas. Expresses the Sense of Congress that the broadband loan program in the Rural Utilities Service should be fully funded. Provides for the expensing of broadband Internet access expenditures for rural communities. Introduced March 2, 2005; referred to Committee on Finance.

S. 502 (Coleman)

Rural Renaissance Act. Creates a Rural Renaissance Corporation which would fund qualified projects including projects to expand broadband technology in rural areas. Introduced March 3, 2005; referred to Committee on Finance.

S. 1147 (Rockefeller)

Amends the Internal Revenue Code of 1986 to provide for the expensing of broadband Internet access expenditures. Introduced May 26, 2005; referred to Committee on Finance.

S. 1321 (Santorum)

Telephone Excise Tax Repeal Act of 2005. Amends the Internal Revenue Code of 1986 to provide for the expensing of broadband Internet access expenditures. Introduced June 28, 2005; reported by Committee on Finance, September 15, 2006 (S.Rept. 109-336).

S. 1583 (Smith)

Universal Service for the 21st Century Act. Amends the Communications Act of 1934 to expand the contribution base for universal service and to establish a separate account — not to exceed $500 million per year — within the universal service fund to support the deployment of broadband service in unserved areas of the United States. Introduced July 29, 2005; referred to Committee on Commerce, Science and Transportation.

S. 1932 (Gregg)

Deficit Reduction Act of 2005. Section 1401 cancels unobligated funds remaining as of October 1, 2006 for the USDA Rural Utilities Service Rural Broadband Access Loan and Loan Guarantee Program. Title III sets a hard deadline for the digital television transition, thereby reclaiming analog television spectrum to be auctioned for commercial applications such as wireless broadband. Passed Senate, November 3, 2005. House agreed to conference report (H.Rept. 109-362), December 19, 2005. Senate agreed to conference report with amendments, December 21, 2005. House agreed to amended conference report, February 1, 2006. **P.L. 109-171** signed by President, February 8, 2006.

S. 1765 (Landrieu)

Louisiana Katrina Reconstruction Act. Provides grants for construction of broadband infrastructure necessary for technology and economic development in areas affected by Hurricane Katrina. Introduced September 22, 2005; referred to Committee on Finance.

S. 1766 (Vitter)

Louisiana Katrina Reconstruction Act. Provides grants for construction of broadband infrastructure necessary for technology and economic development in areas affected by Hurricane Katrina. Introduced September 22, 2005; referred to Committee on Finance.

S. 2020 (Grassley)

Tax Relief Act of 2005. Provides a tax credit to holders of rural renaissance bonds funding qualified projects including expanding broadband technology in rural areas. Passed by Senate as H.R. 4297, February 2, 2006. Provision not retained in Conference Report.

S. 2256 (Burns)

Internet and Universal Service Act of 2006. Amends the Communications Act of 1934 to ensure the availability to all Americans of high-quality, advanced telecommunications and broadband services, technologies, and networks at just, reasonable, and affordable rates, and to establish a permanent mechanism to guarantee specific, sufficient, and predictable support for the preservation and advancement of universal service. Introduced February 8, 2006; referred to Committee on Commerce, Science, and Transportation.

S. 2357 (Kennedy)

Right TRACK Act. Directs the President's Council of Advisors on Science and Technology to establish a national broadband policy for improving and expanding broadband access in the United States by 2010. Introduced March 2, 2006; referred to Committee on Finance.

S. 2686 (Stevens)

Communications, Consumer's Choice, and Broadband Deployment Act of 2006. A bill to amend the Communications Act of 1934 and for other purposes. Includes provision on universal service reform. Introduced May 1, 2006; referred to Committee on Commerce, Science, and Transportation.

S. 3820 (Durbin)

Broadband for Rural America Act of 2006. Establishes a Broadband Access Trust Fund and Office of Broadband Access within the FCC to provide grants to study the lack of affordable broadband in unserved areas. Also reforms FCC's broadband data reporting and USDA's broadband loan and grant programs, provides for spectrum auction for wireless rural broadband, and establishes a public-private Rural Broadband Access Task Force. Introduced August 3, 2006; referred to Committee on Commerce, Science, and Transportation.

S. 3829 (Stabenow)

Tax Relief and Minimum Wage Act of 2006. Provides a tax credit to holders of rural renaissance bonds funding qualified projects including expanding broadband technology in rural areas. Introduced August 3, 2006; referred to Committee on Finance.

S. 3936 (Frist)

National Competitiveness Investment Act. Authorizes the National Science Foundation to provide grants for basic research in advanced information and communications technologies. Areas of research include affordable broadband access, including wireless technologies. Introduced September 26, 2006; placed on Senate Legislative Calendar.

S. 3999 (Clinton)

Rural Broadband Initiative Act of 2006. Establishes an Office of Rural Broadband Initiatives within the Department of Agriculture which will administer all rural broadband grant and loan programs previously administered by the Rural Utilities Service. Also establishes a National Rural Broadband Innovation Fund which would fund experimental and pilot rural broadband projects and applications. Introduced September 29, 2006; placed on Senate Legislative Calendar.

LEGISLATION IN THE 110TH CONGRESS

Many of the legislative proposals related to providing financial assistance for broadband deployment are likely to be reintroduced into the 110th Congress. Of particular note is the possible reauthorization of the Rural Utilities Service (RUS) broadband program, which is expected to be considered as part of the 2007 farm bill. Legislation to reform universal service – which could have a significant impact on the amount of financial assistance available for broadband deployment in rural and underserved areas – has been introduced into the 110th Congress (H.R. 42, S. 101).

H.R. 42 (Velazquez)

Serving Everyone with Reliable, Vital Internet, Communications and Education Act of 2007. Directs the FCC to expand assistance provided by the Lifeline Assistance Program and the Link Up Program to include broadband service. Introduced January 4, 2007; referred to Committee on Energy and Commerce.

S. 101 (Stevens)

Universal Service for Americans Act ("USA Act"). Directs the FCC to establish Broadband for Unserved Area Areas Program to be funded by the Universal Service Fund. Requires communications carriers to submit detailed broadband deployment data to the FCC. Introduced January 4, 2007; referred to Committee on Commerce, Science, and Transportation.

POLICY ISSUES

Legislation in the 110th Congress will likely seek to provide federal financial assistance for broadband deployment in rural and underserved areas. In assessing this legislation, several policy issues arise.

Is Broadband Deployment Data Adequate?

Obtaining an accurate snapshot of the status of broadband deployment is problematic. Anecdotes abound of rural and low-income areas which do not have adequate Internet access, as well as those which are receiving access to high-speed, state-of-the-art connections. Rapidly evolving technologies, the constant flux of the telecommunications industry, the uncertainty of consumer wants and needs, and the sheer diversity and size of the nation's economy and geography make the status of broadband deployment very difficult to characterize. The FCC periodically collects broadband deployment data from the private sector via "FCC Form 477" — a standardized information gathering survey. Statistics derived from the Form 477 survey are published every six months. Additionally, data from Form 477 are used as the basis of the FCC's (to date) four broadband deployment reports. The FCC is working to refine the data used in future Reports in order to provide an increasingly accurate portrayal. In its March 17, 2004 Notice of Inquiry for the *Fourth Report*, the FCC sought comments on specific proposals to improve the FCC Form 477 data gathering program.[56] On November 9, 2004, the FCC voted to expand its data collection program by requiring reports from all facilities based carriers regardless of size in order to better track rural and underserved markets, by requiring broadband providers to provide more information on the speed and nature of their service, and by establishing broadband-over-power line as a separate category in order to track its development and deployment. The FCC Form 477 data gathering program is extended for five years beyond its March 2005 expiration date.[57]

The Government Accountability Office (GAO) has cited concerns about the FCC's zip-code level data. Of particular concern is that the FCC will report broadband service in a zip code even if a company reports service to only one subscriber, which in turn can lead to some observers overstating of broadband deployment. According to GAO, "the data may not provide a highly accurate depiction of local deployment of broadband infrastructures for residential service, especially in rural areas." The FCC has acknowledged the limitations in its zip code level data.[58]

In the 109th Congress, H.R. 5252, the communications reform bill as marked up by the Senate Committee on Commerce, Science and Transportation on June 28, 2006, contained a provision which sought to revise the FCC's broadband data collection program. Section 1011, "Broadband Reporting Requirements," would have required the FCC to collect data by "zip code plus four" service areas. Specifically, the FCC would require data for each service area on the percentage of households offered broadband service, the percentage of households actually subscribing to broadband service, the average price per megabyte of download and upload speeds, actual average throughput speeds, and the ratio of the number of users sharing the same line. Exemptions would be allowed if the FCC determined that a broadband provider's compliance with the reporting requirements was cost prohibitive. Additionally, the

FCC would be directed to provide to Congress an annual report on the demographics of areas not served by any broadband provider.

Is Federal Assistance for Broadband Deployment Premature or Inappropriate?

Related to the data issue is the argument that government intervention in the broadband marketplace would be premature or inappropriate. Some argue that financial assistance for broadband deployment could distort private sector investment decisions in a dynamic and rapidly evolving marketplace, and question whether federal tax dollars should support a technology that has not yet matured, and whose societal benefits have not yet been demonstrated.[59]

On the other hand, proponents of financial assistance counter that the available data show, in general, that the private sector will invest in areas where it expects the greatest return — areas of high population density and income. Without some governmental assistance in underserved areas, they argue, it is reasonable to conclude that broadband deployment will lag behind in many rural and low income areas.[60]

Which Approach Is Best?

If one assumes that governmental action is appropriate to spur broadband deployment in underserved areas, which specific approaches, either separately or in combination, would likely be most effective? Targeted grants and loans from several existing federal programs have been proposed, as well as tax credits for companies deploying broadband systems in rural and low-income areas. How might the impact of federal assistance compare with the effects of regulatory or deregulatory actions?[61] And finally, how might any federal assistance programs best compliment existing "digital divide" initiatives by the states, localities, and private sector?

Table 1. Selected Federal Domestic Assistance Programs Related to Telecommunications Development

Program	Agency	Description	FY2006 (obligations)	Web Links for More Information [http://12.46.245.173/cfda/cfda.html]: Go to "All Programs Listed Numerically" and search by program
Public Telecommunications Facilities — Planning and Construction	National Telecommunications and Information Administration, Dept. of Commerce	Assists in planning, acquisition, installation and modernization of public telecommunications facilities	$19.7 million	[http://www.ntia.doc.gov/otiahome/ptfp/index.html]
Grants for Public Works and Economic Development Facilities	Economic Development Administration, Dept. of Commerce	Provides grants to economically distressed areas for construction of public facilities and infrastructure, including broadband deployment and other types of telecommunications enabling projects	$158.1 million	[http://www.eda.gov/]
Rural Telephone Loans and Loan Guarantees	Rural Utilities Service, U.S. Dept. of Agriculture	Provides long-term direct and guaranteed loans to qualified organizations for the purpose of financing the improvement, expansion, construction, acquisition, and operation of telephone lines, facilities, or systems to furnish and improve telecommunications service in rural areas	$145 million (hardship loans); $420 million (cost of money loans); $175 million (FFB Treasury loans)	[http://www.usda.gov/rus/telecom/index.htm]
Distance Learning and Telemedicine Loans and Grants	Rural Utilities Service, U.S. Dept. of Agriculture	Provides seed money for loans and grants to rural community facilities (e.g., schools, libraries, hospitals) for advanced telecommunications systems that can provide health care and educational benefits to rural areas	$54.4 million (grants) $25 million (loans)	[http://www.usda.gov/rus/telecom/dlt/dlt.htm]

Table 1. (Continued).

Program	Agency	Description	FY2006 (obligations)	Web Links for More Information [http://12.46.245.173/cfda/cfda.html]: Go to "All Programs Listed Numerically" and search by program
Rural Broadband Access Loan and Loan Guarantee Program	Rural Utilities Service, U.S. Dept. of Agriculture	Provides loan and loan guarantees for facilities and equipment providing broadband service in rural communities	$2032 million (cost of money loan) $46 million (4% loan) $79 million (loan guarantee)	[http://www.usda.gov/rus/telecom/broadband.htm]
Community Connect Broadband Grants	Rural Utilities Service, U.S. Dept. of Agriculture	Provides grants to applicants proposing to provide broadband service on a "communityoriented connectivity" basis to rural communities of under 20,000 inhabitants.	$9 million	[http://www.usda.gov/rus/telecom/index.htm]
Education Technology State Grants	Office of Elementary and Secondary Education, Dept. of Education	Grants to State Education Agencies for development of information technology to improve teaching and learning in schools	$272 million	[http://www.ed.gov/Technology/TLCF/index.html]
Star Schools	Office of Assistant Secretary for Educational Research and Improvement, Dept. of Education	Grants to telecommunication partnerships for telecommunications facilities and equipment, educational and instructional programming	$14.8 million	[http://www.ed.gov/programs/starschools/index.html]
Ready to Teach	Office of Assistant Secretary for Educational Research and Improvement, Dept. of Education	Grants to carry out a national telecommunication-based program to improve the teaching in core curriculum areas.	$10.9 million	[http://www.ed.gov/programs/readyteach/index.html]
Special Education — Technology and Media Services for Individuals with Disabilities	Office of Special Education and Rehabilitative Services, Dept. of Education	Supports development and application of technology and education media activities for disabled children and adults	$38.4 million	[http://www.ed.gov/about/offices/list/osers/index.htm l?src=mr/]

Table 1. (Continued).

Program	Agency	Description	FY2006 (obligations)	Web Links for More Information [http://12.46.245.173/cfda/cfda.html]: Go to "All Programs Listed Numerically" and search by program
Telehealth Network Grants	Health Resources and Services Administration, Department of Health and Human Services	Grants to develop sustainable telehealth programs and networks in rural and frontier areas, and in medically unserved areas and populations.	$3.4 million	[http://www.hrsa.gov/telehealth/]
Medical Library Assistance	National Library of Medicine, National Institutes of Health, Department of Health and Human Services	Provides funds to train professional personnel; strengthen library and information services; facilitate access to and delivery of health science information; plan and develop advanced information networks; support certain kinds of biomedical publications; and conduct research in medical informatics and related sciences	$65.2 million	[http://www.nlm.nih.gov/ep/extramural.html]
State Library Program	Office of Library Services, Institute of Museum and Library Services, National Foundation on the Arts and the Humanities	Grants to state library administrative agencies for promotion of library services that provide all users access to information through State, regional, and international electronic networks	$163.7 million	[http://www.imls.gov/grants/library/lib_gsla.asp#po]
Native American and Native Hawaiian Library Services	Office of Library Services, Institute of Museum and Library Services, National Foundation on the Arts and the Humanities	Supports library services including electronically linking libraries to networks	$3.6 million	[http://www.imls.gov/grants/library/lib_nat.asp]

Table 1. (Continued).

Program	Agency	Description	FY2006 (obligations)	Web Links for More Information [http://12.46.245.173/cfda/cfda.html]: Go to "All Programs Listed Numerically" and search by program
Appalachian Area Development	Appalachian Regional Commission	Provides project grants for Appalachian communities to support the physical infrastructure necessary for economic development and improved quality of life.	$62 million	[http://www.arc.gov/index.do?nodeId=21]
Denali Commission Program	Denali Commission	Provides grants through a federal and state partnership designed to provide critical infrastructure and utilities throughout Alaska, particularly in distressed communities	$139 million	[http://www.denali.gov/]

Prepared by CRS based on information from the Catalog of Federal Domestic Assistance, updated December 2006.

REFERENCES

[1]   The term "digital divide" can also refer to international disparities in access to information technology. This report focuses on domestic issues only.

[2]   See U.S. Department of Commerce, *Falling Through the Net: Toward Digital Inclusion*, released October 2000.

[3]   Not all observers agree that a "digital divide" exists. See, for example: Thierer, Adam D., *Divided Over the Digital Divide*, Heritage Foundation, March 1, 2000. [http://www.heritage.org/Press/Commentary/ED030100.cfm]

[4]   Department of Commerce, *A Nation Online: How Americans Are Expanding Their Use of the Internet*, February 2002. Based on a September 2001 Census Bureau survey of 57,000 households. See [http://www.ntia.doc.gov/ntiahome/dn/index.html]

[5]   A Nation Online, pp. 10-11.

[6]   For further information on different types of broadband technologies, including their respective strengths and limitations, see CRS Report RL33542, *Broadband Internet Access: Background and Issues*, by Angele A. Gilroy and Lennard G. Kruger.

[7]   U.S. Department of Commerce, Economics and Statistics Administration, National Telecommunications and Information Administration, *A Nation Online: Entering the Broadband Age*, September 2004, p. 1.

[8]   FCC, High-Speed Services for Internet Access: Status as of June 30, 2006, January 2007. Available at [http://hraunfoss.fcc.gov/edocs_public/attachmatch/DOC-270128A1.pdf]

[9]   U.S. Government Accountability Office, Broadband Deployment is Extensive throughout the United States, but It Is Difficult to Assess the Extent of Deployment Gaps in Rural Areas, GAO-06-426, May 2006, p. 3.

[10]   Federal Communications Commission, *Fourth Report to Congress*, "Availability of Advanced Telecommunications Capability in the United States," GN Docket No. 04-54, FCC 04-208, September 9, 2004, p. 38. Available at [http://hraunfoss.fcc.gov/edocs_public/attachmatch/FCC-04-208A1.pdf]

[11]   For more information on rural broadband and broadband programs at the Rural Utilities Service, see CRS Report RL33816, *Broadband Loan and Grant Programs in the USDA's Rural Utilities Service, by* Lennard G. Kruger.

[12]   See U.S. Depts. of Commerce and Agriculture, *Advanced Telecommunications in Rural America: The Challenge of Bringing Broadband Service to All Americans*, April 2000, 80 pages. Available at [http://www.ntia.doc.gov/reports/ruralbb42600.pdf]

[13]   A Nation Online, pp. 40-41.

[14]   Horrigan, John B., Pew Internet and American Life Project, *Rural Broadband Internet Use,* February 2006, Available at [http://www.pewinternet.org/ pdfs/PIP_Rural_Broadband.pdf]

[15]   U.S. Government Accountability Office, Broadband Deployment is Extensive throughout the United States, but It Is Difficult to Assess the Extent of Deployment Gaps in Rural Areas, GAO-06-426, May 2006, p. 12.

[16]   FCC, *High-Speed Services for Internet Access: Status as of June 30, 2006,* January 2007, p. 4. Available at [http://hraunfoss.fcc.gov/edocs_public/attachmatch/DOC-270128A1.pdf]

[17]   Fourth Report, p. 8-9.

[18]   A Nation Online: Entering the Broadband Age, pp. 12-13.

[19]   *Ibid.*, p. 12.

[20]   *Ibid.*, p. A-1.

[21]   Crandall, Robert W. et al, *The Effect of Ubiquitous Broadband Adoption on Investment, Jobs, and the U.S. Economy*, Conducted by Criterion Economics, L.L.C. for the New Millennium Research Council, September 2003. Available at [http://www. newmillenniumresearch.org/archive/bbstudyreport_091703.pdf]

[22]   Gillett, Sharon E., Massachusetts Institute of Technology, "Measuring Broadband's Economic Impact," report prepared for the Economic Development Administration, U.S. Department of Commerce, February 28, 2006 p. 4.

[23]   International Telecommunications Union, Economies by broadband penetration, 2005. Available at [http://www.itu.int/ITU-D/ict/statistics/at_glance/top20_broad_2005.html].

[24]   OECD, *OECD Broadband Statistics, June 2006*. Available at [http://www.oecd.org/ document/9/0,2340,en_2649_34223_37529673_1_1_1_1,00.html]

[25]   OECD, Directorate for Science, Technology and Industry, *The Development of Broadband Access in OECD Countries*, October 29, 2001, 63 pages. For a comparison of government broadband policies, also see OECD, Directorate for Science, Technology and Industry, *Broadband Infrastructure Deployment: The Role of Government Assistance*, May 22, 2002, 42 pages.

[26]   FCC News Release, "FCC Issues Report on the Deployment of Advanced Telecommunications Capability to All Americans," January 28, 1999. [http://www.fcc.gov/Bureaus/Common_Carrier/News_Releases/1999/nrcc9004.html]

[27]   Deployment of Advanced Telecommunications Capability: Second Report, p. 6.

[28]   Third Report, p. 5.

[29]   *Ibid.*, p. 5-6.

[30]   Fourth Report, p. 8.

[31]   *Ibid.*, p. 9.

[32]   *Ibid.*, p. 5, 7.

[33]   See Appendix C of the *Fourth Report*, "List of Broadband-Related Proceedings at the Commission," pp. 54-56.

[34]   See speech by Nancy Victory, Assistant Secretary for Communications and Information, before the National Summit on Broadband Deployment, October 25, 2001, [http://www.ntia.doc.gov/ntiahome/speeches/2001/broadband_102501.htm]

[35]   Address by Nancy Victory, NTIA Administrator, before the Alliance for Public Technology Broadband Symposium, February 8, 2002, [http://www.ntia.doc.gov/ ntiahome/speeches/2002/apt_020802.htm]

[36]   See White House, *A New Generation of American Innovation*, April 2004. Available at [http://www.whitehouse.gov/infocus/technology/economic_policy200404/innovation.p df]

[37]   Available at [http://www.technology.gov/reports/TechPolicy/Broadband_020921.pdf]

[38]   President's Council of Advisors on Science and Technology, Office of Science and Technology Policy, *Building Out Broadband*, December 2002, 14 p. Available at [http://www.ostp.gov/PCAST/FINAL%20Broadband%20Report%20With%20Letters.p df]

[39] TechNet represents over 300 senior executives from companies in the fields of information technology, biotechnology, venture capital, investment banking, and law. TechNet's policy document, "A National Imperative: Universal Availability of Broadband by 2010," is available at [http://www.technet.org/news/release/?postId= 6265 and pageTitle=TechNet+CEOs+Call+for+National+Broadband+Policy]

[40] CSPP is composed of nine CEOs from computer hardware and information technology companies. See "A Vision for 21st Century Wired and Wireless Broadband: Building the Foundation of the Networked World," [http://www.cspp.org/documents /networkedworld.pdf]

[41] See Semiconductor Industry Association, "Removing Barriers to Broadband Deployment," [http://www.sia-online.org/downloads/Broadband_Combined.pdf]

[42] American Electronics Association, *Broadband in the States 2003: A State-by-State Overview of Broadband Deployment*, May 22, 2003. [http://www.aeanet.org/ publications/idet_broadbandstates03.asp]

[43] TechNet, *The State Broadband Index: An Assessment of State Policies Impacting Broadband Deployment and Demand*, July 17, 2003, 48 p. Available at [http://www.michigan.gov/documents/State_Broadband_Index_71282_7.pdf]

[44] Alliance for Public Technology, *A Nation of Laboratories: Broadband Policy Experiments in the States*, March 5, 2004, 48 p. Available at [http://www.apt.org /publications/reports-studies/broadbandreport_final.pdf]

[45] California Public Utilities Commission, *Broadband Deployment in California*, May 5, 2005, 83 p. Available at [http://www.cpuc.ca.gov/static/telco/ reports/ broadbandreport. htm]

[46] Wallsten, Scott, AEI-Brookings Joint Center for Regulatory Studies, *Broadband Penetration: An Empirical Analysis of State and Federal Policies*, Working Paper 05-12, June 2005, 29 p. Available at[http://aei-brookings.org/admin/authorpdfs/ page.php?id=1161]

[47] The section on universal service was prepared by Angele Gilroy, Specialist in Telecommunications, Resources, Science and Industry Division.

[48] Communications Act of 1934, As Amended, Title I sec.1[47 U.S.C. 151].

[49] Many states participate in or have programs that mirror FCC universal service mechanisms to help promote universal service goals within their states.

[50] Additional FCC policies such as rate averaging and pooling have also been implemented to assist high cost carriers.

[51] For additional information on this program, including funding commitments, see the E-rate website: [http://www.universalservice.org/sl/]

[52] Any health care provider that does not have toll-free access to the Internet can receive the lesser of $180 in toll charges per month or the toll charges incurred for 30 hours of access to the Internet per month. To obtain this support the health care provider does not have to be located in a rural area, but must show that it lacks toll-free Internet access and that it is an eligible health care provider.

[53] For additional information on this program, including funding commitments, see the RHCD website: [http://www.universalservice.org/rhc/]

[54] The TDF also provides management and technical assistance to the companies in which it invests.

[55] For additional information on this program see the TDF website at [http://www.tdfund.com]

[56] Federal Communications Commission, *Notice of Inquiry*, "Concerning the Deployment of Advanced Telecommunications Capability to All Americans in a Reasonable and Timely Fashion, and possible Steps to Accelerate Such Deployment Pursuant to Section 706 of the Telecommunications Act of 1996," FCC 04-55, March 17, 2004, p. 6.

[57] FCC News Release, *FCC Improves Data Collection to Monitor Nationwide Broadband Rollout*, November 9, 2004. Available at [http://hraunfoss.fcc.gov/edocs_public/attachmatch/DOC-254115A1.pdf]

[58] U.S. Government Accountability Office, Broadband Deployment is Extensive throughout the United States, but It Is Difficult to Assess the Extent of Deployment Gaps in Rural Areas, GAO-06-426, May 2006, p. 3.

[59] See Leighton, Wayne A., *Broadband Deployment and the Digital Divide: A Primer*, a Cato Institute Policy Analysis, No. 410, August 7, 2001, 34 pp. Available at [http://www.cato.org/pubs/pas/pa410.pdf]. Also see Thierer, Adam, *Broadband Tax Credits, the High-Tech Pork Barrel Begins*, Cato Institute, July 13, 2001, available at [http://www.cato.org/tech/tk/010713-tk.html].

[60] See for example: Cooper, Mark, Consumer Federation of America and Consumers Union, *Expanding the Digital Divide and Falling Behind on Broadband*, October 2004, 33 pages. Available at [http://www.consumersunion.org/pub/ddnewbook.pdf]

[61] See CRS Report RL33542, *Broadband Internet Access: Background and Issues*, by Angele A. Gilroy and Lennard G. Kruger, for a discussion of regulatory issues.

In: Broadband Internet: Access, Regulation and Policy
Editor: Ellen S. Cohen, pp. 77-94
ISBN: 978-1-60456-073-2
© 2007 Nova Science Publishers, Inc.

Chapter 4

BROADBAND INTERNET REGULATION AND ACCESS: BACKGROUND AND ISSUES[*]

Angele A. Gilroy[1] and Lennard G. Kruger[2]

[1] Telecommunications Resources, Science, and Industry Division
[2] Science and Technology Resources, Science, and Industry Division

ABSTRACT

Broadband or high-speed Internet access is provided by a series of technologies that give users the ability to send and receive data at volumes and speeds far greater than current Internet access over traditional telephone lines. In addition to offering speed, broadband access provides a continuous, "always on" connection and the ability to both receive (download) and transmit (upload) data at high speeds. Broadband access, along with the content and services it might enable, has the potential to transform the Internet: both what it offers and how it is used. It is likely that many of the future applications that will best exploit the technological capabilities of broadband have yet to be developed. There are multiple transmission media or technologies that can be used to provide broadband access. These include cable, an enhanced telephone service called digital subscriber line (DSL), satellite, fixed wireless (including "wi-fi" and "Wi-Max"), broadband over powerline (BPL), fiber-to-the-home (FTTH), and others. While many (though not all) offices and businesses now have Internet broadband access, a remaining challenge is providing broadband over "the last mile" to consumers in their homes. Currently, a number of competing telecommunications companies are developing, deploying, and marketing specific technologies and services that provide residential broadband access.

From a public policy perspective, the goals are to ensure that broadband deployment is timely and contributes to the nation's economic growth, that industry competes fairly, and that service is provided to all sectors and geographical locations of American society. The federal government — through Congress and the Federal Communications Commission (FCC) — is seeking to ensure fair competition among the players so that broadband will be available and affordable in a timely manner to all Americans who want it.

---

[*] Excerpted from CRS Report RL33542, dated September 18, 2006.

While President Bush has set a goal of universal broadband availability by 2007, some areas of the nation — particularly rural and low-income communities —continue to lack full access to high-speed broadband Internet service. In order to address this problem, the 109th Congress is examining the scope and effect of federal broadband financial assistance programs (including universal service), and the impact of telecommunications regulation and new technologies on broadband deployment. One facet of the debate over broadband services focuses on whether present laws and subsequent regulatory policies are needed to ensure the development of competition and its subsequent consumer benefits, or conversely, whether such laws and regulations are overly burdensome and discourage needed investment in and deployment of broadband services. The Congressional debate has focused on H.R. 5252 which addresses a number of issues, including the extent to which legacy regulations should be applied to traditional providers as they enter new markets, the extent to which legacy regulations should be imposed on new entrants as they compete with traditional providers in their markets, the treatment of new and converging technologies, and the emergence of municipal broadband networks and Internet access. This report — which will be updated as events warrant — replaces CRS Issue Brief IB10045, *Broadband Internet Regulation and Access: Background and Issues.*

MOST RECENT DEVELOPMENTS

In the 109th Congress, legislation has been introduced to provide financial assistance to encourage broadband deployment (H.R. 144, H.R. 146, H.R. 1479, H.R. 3517, H.R. 3958, H.R. 4297, H.R. 5970, S. 14, S. 497, S. 502, S. 1147, S. 1583, S. 1765, S. 1766, S. 3820, S. 3829). Also, the impact of existing laws and regulatory policies on broadband providers and ultimately broadband deployment continues to be of congressional interest in the second session (H.R. 214, H.R. 2726, H.R. 3146, H.R. 5252, H.R. 5273, H.R. 5417, S. 1294, S. 1349, S. 1504, S. 1583, S. 2113, S. 2256, S. 2360, S. 2686, S. 2917, S. 2989).

The House Energy and Commerce Committee on April 26, 2006, passed (42-12), with amendment, H.R. 5252, a comprehensive telecommunications bill. The measure, entitled the "Communications Opportunity, Promotion, and Enhancement Act" (COPE), was the subject of a sequential referral request, by House Judiciary Chairman Sensenbrenner, which delayed floor consideration. That referral request was denied. The House Rules Committee approved eight amendments to be considered during floor debate on H.R. 5252. The House passed (321-101) H.R. 5252, with amendment, on June 8, 2006.

Senate Commerce Committee Chairman Stevens introduced, on May 1, 2006, a major telecommunications bill, S. 2686, which was the topic of Committee hearings on May 18, and May 25, 2006. A revised draft of the bill was the subject of a June 13, 2006 Committee hearing. A third revision was passed (15-7) with amendment, by the Commerce Committee on June 28, 2006. After a lengthy and intense markup the Senate Commerce Committee approved (15-7) on June 28, 2006 the newly titled "Advanced Telecommunications and Opportunity Reform Act," (ATOR), which technically is an amended version in the nature of a substitute for H.R. 5252. In addition to a new bill name and number the three-day markup led to the approval of a significant manager's amendment containing a new title and 70 amendments resulting in the passage of a 200-plus page omnibus telecommunications measure. S. 2686, which is now referred to as "the Senate Committee passed version of H.R.

5252," or H.R. 5252 (ATOR) is still pending in Committee. It remains uncertain if the measure will be considered by the Senate.

Both the Senate and House Judiciary Committees have also announced intentions to examine issues related to telecommunications reform. The House Judiciary's Telecommunications and Antitrust Task Force held a hearing, on April 25, 2006, to examine competition issues relating to Internet access and "net neutrality." Chairman Sensenbrenner and Representative Conyers introduced, on May 18, 2006, a bipartisan bill (H.R. 5417) addressing the issue of Internet access, which was passed (20-13) as amended, by the full committee on May 25, 2006. The Senate Judiciary Committee held a June 14, 2006 hearing on communications laws and ensuring competition and innovation.

BACKGROUND AND ANALYSIS

Broadband or high-speed Internet access is provided by a series of technologies that give users the ability to send and receive data at volumes and speeds far greater than current Internet access over traditional telephone lines. Currently, a number of telecommunications companies are developing, installing, and marketing specific technologies and services to provide broadband access to the home. Meanwhile, the federal government — through Congress and the Federal Communications Commission (FCC) — is seeking to ensure fair competition among the players so that broadband will be available and affordable in a timely manner to all Americans who want it.

What Is Broadband and Why Is It Important?

Traditionally, Internet users have accessed the Internet through the same telephone line that can be used for traditional voice communication. A personal computer equipped with a modem is used to hook into an Internet dial-up connection provided (for a fee) by an Internet service provider (ISP) of choice. The modem converts analog signals (voice) into digital signals that enable the transmission of "bits" of data.

The faster the data transmission rate, the faster one can download files or hop from Web page to Web page. The highest speed modem used with a traditional telephone line, known as a 56K modem, offers a maximum data transmission rate of about 45,000 bits per second (bps). However, as the content on the World Wide Web becomes more sophisticated, the limitations of relatively low data transmission rates (called "narrowband") such as 56K become apparent. For example, using a 56K modem connection to download a 10-minute video or a large software file can be a lengthy and frustrating exercise. By using a broadband high-speed Internet connection, with data transmission rates many times faster than a 56K modem, users can view video, make telephone calls, or download software and other data-rich files in a matter of seconds. In addition to offering speed, broadband access provides a continuous "always on" connection (no need to "dial-up") and a "two-way" capability — that is, the ability to both receive (download) and transmit (upload) data at high speeds.

Broadband access, along with the content and services it might enable, has the potential to transform the Internet — both what it offers and how it is used. For example, a two-way high speed connection could be used for interactive applications such as online classrooms, showrooms, or health clinics, where teacher and student (or customer and salesperson, doctor and patient) can see and hear each other through their computers. An "always on" connection could be used to monitor home security, home automation, or even patient health remotely through the Web. The high speed and high volume that broadband offers could also be used for bundled service where, for example, cable television, video on demand, voice, data, and other services are all offered over a single line. In truth, it is possible that many of the applications that will best exploit the technological capabilities of broadband, while also capturing the imagination of consumers, have yet to be developed.

Broadband Technologies

There are multiple transmission media or technologies that can be used to provide broadband access. These include cable modem, an enhanced telephone service called digital subscriber line (DSL), satellite technology, terrestrial (or fixed) wireless technologies, and others. Cable and DSL are currently the most widely used technologies for providing broadband access. Both require the modification of an existing physical infrastructure that is already connected to the home (i.e., cable television and telephone lines). Each technology has its respective advantages and disadvantages, and will likely compete with each other based on performance, price, quality of service, geography, user friendliness, and other factors. The following sections summarize cable, DSL, and other prospective broadband technologies.

Cable
The same cable network that currently provides television service to consumers is being modified to provide broadband access. Because cable networks are shared by users, access speeds can decrease during peak usage hours, when bandwidth is being shared by many customers at the same time. Network sharing has also led to security concerns and fears that hackers might be able to eavesdrop on a neighbor's Internet connection. The cable industry is developing "next generation" technology which will significantly extend downloading and uploading speeds.

Digital Subscriber Line (DSL)
DSL is a modem technology that converts existing copper telephone lines into two-way high speed data conduits. Speeds can depend on the condition of the telephone wire and the distance between the home and the telephone company's central office (i.e., the building that houses telephone switching equipment). Because DSL uses frequencies much higher than those used for voice communication, both voice and data can be sent over the same telephone line. Thus, customers can talk on their telephone while they are online, and voice service will continue even if the DSL service goes down. Like cable broadband technology, a DSL line is "always on" with no dial-up required. Unlike cable, however, DSL has the advantage of being unshared between the customer and the central office. Thus, data transmission speeds will not necessarily decrease during periods of heavy local Internet use. A disadvantage relative to cable is that DSL deployment is constrained by the distance between the subscriber and the central office. DSL technology over a copper wire only works within 18,000 feet (about three

miles) of a central office facility. However, DSL providers are deploying technology to further increase deployment range. One option is to install "remote terminals" which can serve areas farther than three miles from the central office.

Wireless

Terrestrial or fixed wireless systems transmit data over the airwaves from towers or antennas to a receiver. Mobile wireless broadband services (also referred to as third generation or "3G") allow consumers to get broadband access over cell phones, PDAs, or wireless modem cards connected to a laptop.[1] The FCC is planning to auction frequencies currently occupied by broadcast channels 52-69. These and other frequencies in the 700 MHZ band are possible candidates for wireless broadband applications. A number of wireless technologies, corresponding to different parts of the electromagnetic spectrum, also have potential. These include the upperbands (above 24GHz), the lowerbands (multipoint distribution service or MDS, below 3 GHz), broadband personal communications services (PCS), wireless communications service (2.3 GHz), and unlicenced spectrum. Unlicensed spectrum is being increasingly used to provide high-speed short-distance wireless access (popularly called "wi-fi") to local area networks, particularly in urban areas where wired broadband connections already exist. A new and developing wireless broadband technology (called "WiMax") has the capability to transmit signals over much larger areas.

Fiber

Another broadband technology is optical fiber to the home (FTTH). Optical fiber cable, already used by businesses as high speed links for long distance voice and data traffic, has tremendous data capacity, with transmission speeds dramatically higher than what is offered by cable modem or DSL broadband technology. While the high cost of installing optical fiber in or near users' homes has been a major barrier to the deployment of FTTH, both Verizon and AT and T (formerly SBC) are rolling out fiber-based architectures that will offer consumers voice, video, and high-speed data (sometimes referred to as a "triple play"). Some public utilities are also exploring or beginning to offer broadband access via fiber inside their existing conduits. Additionally, some companies are investigating the feasibility of transmitting data over power lines, which are already ubiquitous in people's homes.[2]

Satellite

Satellite broadband Internet service is currently being offered by two providers: Hughes Network Systems (DirecWay) and Starband Communications Inc. Like cable, satellite is a shared medium, meaning that privacy may be compromised and performance speeds may vary depending upon the volume of simultaneous use. Another disadvantage of Internet - over-satellite is its susceptibility to disruption in bad weather. On the other hand, the big advantage of satellite is its universal availability. Whereas cable or DSL is not available to some parts of the United States, satellite connections can be accessed by anyone with a satellite dish facing the southern sky. This makes satellite Internet access a possible solution for rural or remote areas not served by other technologies.

Status of Broadband Deployment

Broadband technologies are currently being deployed by the private sector throughout the United States. According to the latest FCC data on the deployment of high-speed Internet connections (released July 2006), as of December 31, 2005 there were 50.2 million high speed lines connecting homes and businesses to the Internet in the United States, a growth rate of 18% during the second half of 2005.

Of the 50.2 million high speed lines reported by the FCC, 42.9 million serve residential users.[3] As of June 30, 2005, the FCC found at least one high-speed subscriber in 98% of all zip codes in the United States. While the broadband *adoption* rate stands at 28% of U.S. households[4], broadband *availability* is much higher. The FCC estimates that roughly 20 percent of consumers with access to advanced telecommunications capability actually subscribe. According to the FCC, possible reasons for the gap between broadband availability and subscribership include the lack of computers in some homes, price of broadband service, lack of content, and the availability of broadband at work.[5]

According to the International Telecommunications Union, the U.S. ranks 16th worldwide in broadband penetration (subscriptions per 100 inhabitants as of December 2005).[6] Similarly, data from the Organization for Economic Cooperation and Development (OECD) found the U.S. ranking 12th among OECD nations in broadband access per 100 inhabitants as of December 2005.[7] By contrast, in 2001 an OECD study found the U.S. ranking 4th in broadband subscribership per 100 inhabitants (after Korea, Sweden, and Canada).[8]

Access to Broadband and the "Digital Divide"

While the number of new broadband subscribers continues to grow, the rate of broadband deployment in urban and high income areas appears to be outpacing deployment in rural and low-income areas. According to the latest FCC data on the deployment of high-speed Internet connections (released July 2006), high-speed subscribers were reported in 99% of the most densely populated zip codes, as opposed to 88% of zip codes with the lowest population densities. Similarly, for zip codes ranked by median family income, high-speed subscribers were reported present in 99% of the top one-tenth of zip codes, as compared to 90% of the bottom one-tenth of zip codes.[9]

Some policymakers assert that disparities in broadband access across American society could have adverse consequences on those left behind. Many believe that advanced Internet applications of the future — voice over the Internet protocol (VoIP) or high quality video, for example — and the resulting ability for businesses and consumers to engage in e-commerce, may increasingly depend on high speed broadband connections to the Internet. Thus, some say, communities and individuals without access to broadband could be at risk to the extent that e-commerce becomes a critical factor in determining future economic development and prosperity.

FCC Activities

The Telecommunications Act of 1996 (P.L. 104-104) addressed the issue of whether the federal government should intervene to prevent a "digital divide" in broadband access. Section 706 requires the FCC to determine whether "advanced telecommunications capability [i.e., broadband or high-speed access] is being deployed to all Americans in a reasonable and timely fashion." If this is not the case, the act directs the FCC to "take immediate action to accelerate deployment of such capability by removing barriers to infrastructure investment and by promoting competition in the telecommunications market."

On September 9, 2004, the FCC adopted and released its *Fourth Report* pursuant to Section 706. Like the previous three reports, the FCC concluded that "the overall goal of section 706 is being met, and that advanced telecommunications capability is indeed being deployed on a reasonable and timely basis to all Americans."[10] While the FCC is currently implementing or actively considering some regulatory activities related to broadband,[11] no major regulatory intervention pursuant to Section 706 of the Telecommunications Act of 1996 has been deemed necessary by the FCC at this time.

The FCC noted the future promise of emerging multiple advanced broadband networks which can complement one another:

> For example, in urban and suburban areas, wireless broadband services may "fill in the gaps" in wireline broadband coverage, while wireless and satellite services may bring high-speed broadband to remote areas where wireline deployment may be costly. Having multiple advanced networks will also promote competition in price, features, and quality-of-service among broadband-access providers.[12]

Two FCC Commissioners (Michael Copps and Jonathan Adelstein) dissented from the *Fourth Report* conclusion that broadband deployment is reasonable and timely. They argued that the relatively poor world ranking of United States broadband penetration indicates that deployment is insufficient, that the FCC's continuing definition of broadband as 200 kilobits per second is outdated and is not comparable to the much higher speeds available to consumers in other countries, and that the use of zip code data (measuring the presence of at least one broadband subscriber within a zip code area) does not sufficiently characterize the availability of broadband across geographic areas.[13]

The Government Accountability Office (GAO) has also cited concerns about the FCC's zip code level data. Of particular concern is that the FCC will report broadband service in a zip code even if a company reports service to only one subscriber, which in turn can lead to some observers overstating of broadband deployment. According to GAO, "the data may not provide a highly accurate depiction of local deployment of broadband infrastructures for residential service, especially in rural areas."[14]

Administration Activities

The National Telecommunications and Information Administration (NTIA) at the Department of Commerce (DOC) has been tasked with developing the Bush Administration's broadband policy.[15] Statements from Administration officials indicated that much of the policy would focus on removing regulatory roadblocks to investment in broadband deployment.[16] On June 13, 2002, in a speech at the 21st Century High Tech Forum, President Bush declared that the nation must be aggressive about the expansion of broadband, and cited ongoing activities at the FCC as important in eliminating hurdles and barriers to get broadband implemented. President Bush made similar remarks citing the economic importance of broadband deployment at the August 13, 2002 economic forum in Waco, Texas. Subsequently, a more formal Administration broadband policy was unveiled in March and April of 2004. On March 26, 2004, President Bush endorsed the goal of universal broadband access by 2007.[17] Then on April 26, 2004, President Bush announced a broadband initiative which advocates permanently prohibiting all broadband taxes, making spectrum available for wireless broadband, creating technical standards for broadband over power lines, and simplifying rights-of-way processes on federal lands for broadband providers.[18]

The Bush Administration has also emphasized the importance of encouraging demand for broadband services. On September 23, 2002, the DOC's Office of Technology Policy released a report, *Understanding Broadband Demand: A Review of Critical Issues*,[19] which argues that national governments can accelerate broadband demand by taking a number of steps, including protecting intellectual property, supporting business investment, developing e-government applications, promoting efficient radio spectrum management, and others. Similarly, the President's Council of Advisors on Science and Technology (PCAST) was tasked with studying "demand-side" broadband issues and suggesting policies to stimulate broadband deployment and economic recovery. The PCAST report, *Building Out Broadband*, released in December 2002, concludes that while government should not intervene in the telecommunications marketplace, it should apply existing policies and work with the private sector to promote broadband applications and usage. Specific initiatives include increasing e-government broadband applications (including homeland security); promoting telework, distance learning, and telemedicine; pursuing broadband-friendly spectrum policies; and ensuring access to public rights of way for broadband infrastructure.[20]

Enacted Legislation

Some policymakers in Congress have asserted that the federal government should play a more active role to avoid a "digital divide" in broadband access, and that legislation is necessary to ensure fair competition and timely broadband deployment. The Farm Security and Rural Investment Act of 2002 — signed into law on May 13, 2002 as P.L. 107-171 — contained a provision (Section 6103) authorizing the Secretary of Agriculture to make loans and loan guarantees to eligible entities for facilities and equipment providing broadband service in rural communities. P.L. 107-171 authorized two programs currently being administered by the Rural Utilities Service at the Department of Agriculture: the Rural Broadband Access Loan and Loan Guarantee Program and Community Connect Broadband Grants.[21]

Regulation and Broadband: Convergence and the Changing Marketplace

Rapid technological advances and the resulting convergence of telecommunications providers and markets has prompted the reexamination of the existing telecommunications industry regulatory framework. The "Telecommunications Act of 1996," (P.L.104-104) redefined and recast the 1934 Communications Act to address the emergence of competition in what were previously considered to be monopolistic markets. Despite its relatively recent enactment, however, a consensus has been growing that the modifications brought about by the implementation of the 1996 Act are not sufficient to address the Nation's changing telecommunications environment. Technological changes such as the advancement of Internet technology to supply data, voice, and video as well as the growing convergence in the telecommunications sector, have, according to many policymakers, made it necessary to consider another "rewrite" or revision of the laws governing these markets.

The regulatory debate focuses on a number of issues including the extent to which existing regulations should be applied to traditional providers as they enter new markets where they do not hold market power, the extent to which existing regulations should be imposed on new entrants as they compete with traditional providers in the same markets, and the appropriate regulatory framework to be imposed on new and/or converging technologies that are not easily classified under the present framework.[22]

The regulatory treatment of broadband technologies continues to hold a major focus in the policy debate. A major facet of the debate centers on whether present laws and regulations are needed to ensure the development of competition and its subsequent consumer benefits, or, conversely, whether such laws and policies are overly burdensome and discourage needed investment and deployment of such services. What if any role regulators should play to ensure the Internet remains open to all, often referred to as "open access" requirements or "net neutrality," is also a major and contentious part of the dialogue.[23] In addition to the debate over economic regulation, concern over how and to what extent "social regulations" such as emergency 911 access, disability access, and law enforcement regulations, should be applied to new and converging technologies continues to be debated. The continued growth and expressed interest in municipal broadband networks has also focused debate on what the appropriate role of the government sector should be and whether it should be competing with the private sector.

How traditional policy goals, such as the advancement of universal service mandates, should be revised to accommodate the changing marketplace has also come under scrutiny. For example, issues such as who should receive and who should contribute to universal service funds and whether the definition of universal service objectives should be expanded to include new technologies such as broadband continue to be debated.

Activities in the 109th Congress

In the 109th Congress, legislation has been introduced to provide financial assistance to encourage broadband deployment (H.R. 144, H.R. 146, H.R. 1479, H.R. 3517, H.R. 3958, H.R. 4297, H.R. 5970, S. 14, S. 497, S. 502, S. 1147, S. 1583, S. 1765, S. 1766, S. 2256, S. 3820, S. 3829). In particular, the impact of existing laws and regulatory policies on broadband providers and ultimately broadband deployment continues to be of Congressional interest in the Second Session (H.R. 214, H.R. 2726, H.R. 3146, H.R. 5252, H.R. 5273, H.R. 5417, S. 1294, S. 1349, S. 1504, S. 1583, S. 2113, S. 2256, S. 2360, S. 2686, S. 2917, S. 2989).

H.R. 5252

House Commerce Committee Chairman Barton, on March 27, 2006, released a draft telecommunications reform proposal that was the subject of a Committee hearing on March 30, 2006. The then unnumbered measure, passed (27-4) the subcommittee, with amendment, on April 5, 2006, and passed (42-12) the full Committee with amendment, on April 26, 2006. The measure, titled "The Communications Opportunity, Promotion, and Enhancement Act of 2006" (COPE), was referred to the House Committee on Energy and Commerce and formally introduced as H.R. 5252. A sequential referral request, by House Judiciary Chairman

Sensenbrenner, which was subsequently denied, delayed floor consideration. The House Rules Committee has approved eight amendments to be considered during floor debate. The House passed (321-101) an amended version of H.R. 5252 on June 8, 2006. In addition to a manager's amendment clarifying franchising provisions, five additional amendments were passed. The other amendments: establish a complaint process to resolve fee disputes between a local franchise authority and a cable operator; increase the income discrimination penalty for a cable operator from $500,000 to $750,000; allow a cable franchising authority to issue an order requiring compliance with FCC revised consumer protection rules; preserve FCC authority to require VOIP providers to contribute to the federal universal service fund, when they connect directly or indirectly to the public switched network and compensate network owners for use of their network; and clarification that language in HR5252 giving the FCC the exclusive authority to adjudicate network neutrality does not remove antitrust authority over net neutrality complaints. Two amendments did not pass. The first, an amendment, sponsored by Representative Markey, to strengthen net neutrality provisions failed by a vote of 152-269. The second, to reduce, from 1 percent to 0.5 percent, the fee paid to local franchise authorities relating to PEG/iNet support by women-owned, small business and socially and economically disadvantaged firms was withdrawn.

H.R. 5252 contains provisions that establish a national cable franchising process; clarify the FCC's authority to enforce its network neutrality principles; address VoIP 911 interconnection and E911 requirements; and bar states from prohibiting municipalities from providing their own broadband networks. More specifically, Title I establishes a national process, through the FCC, for new entrants to offer pay TV services and opens it up to incumbent cable providers, once they face local competition. An operator of a national franchise is prohibited from discriminating in the provision of service to any group of residential subscribers based on the income of that group. National consumer protection rules are established with a local authority/FCC complaint procedure. Additional provisions in Title I preserve the local five percent franchise fee cap, preserve and support PEG channel and I-Nets or Institutional Networks (a one percent gross revenue fee is established to ensure financial support), and preserve rights-of-way requirements. The bill also contains provisions to assist small and rural carriers in the provision of video service by allowing video operators to share a headend transmission facility.

Title II clarifies the FCC's authority to enforce its August 2005 network neutrality principles in complaint proceedings, but prohibits the FCC from engaging in related-rulemaking. Fines up to $500,000 per violation are established and the FCC is required to resolve complaints within 90 days. The FCC is also directed to conduct and submit to the House Energy and Commerce and Senate Commerce Committees, within 180 days of enactment, a study, to evaluate ".... whether the objectives of the (FCC's) broadband policy statement and the principles incorporated therein are being achieved."

The remaining four titles deal with a wide range of telecommunications issues. Title III of the bill contains provisions to establish 911 and E-911 requirements for VoIP services that connect to the public switched network and represent a replacement telephone service. Additional provisions provide access to the nation's 911 infrastructure and requires the FCC to appoint a 911 number administrator. Title IV contains provisions that bar states from prohibiting municipalities from providing their own broadband networks (that is telecommunications, information, or cable services), but also requires that they do not discriminate in favor of, or bestow any advantages to, such entities as compared with other providers of such services. The FCC is tasked with submitting within one year of enactment, a report to Congress, on the status of the provision of such services by municipalities. Titles V and VI contain provisions that ensue consumers can buy stand-alone broadband service; call for an FCC study to examine the possible interference associated with the deployment of broadband over power lines; and further the development of "seamless mobility."

S. 2686

The Senate Commerce Committee has held a series of hearings on a wide range of telecommunications issues in preparation for developing comprehensive telecommunications legislation. Senate Commerce Committee Chairman Stevens introduced, on May 1, 2006, a comprehensive (135 page) telecommunications bill, S. 2686. The major provisions of the measure deal with a wide range of topics, including universal service reform; streamlining of the video franchising process; requiring the FCC to report annually to Congress on the net neutrality issue; interoperability of public safety communications systems; interconnection; and municipal broadband ownership. The bill also contains a number of provisions relating to broadcast issues such as the digital television transition, the reinstating of the FCC's "broadcast flag" rules, access to sports programming, and use of unlicensed "white space." Additional provisions relating to protecting children from child pornography and amending the FCC's "sunshine rules" are also included.

Although Senator Inouye, the ranking minority member of the Committee, signed on as a bill co-sponsor, he has stated that S. 2686 needs considerable amendment to gain his support. He is circulating a draft proposal containing provisions addressing video franchising, Internet access, broadband deployment, and universal service, for consideration that addresses his concerns. The lack of a strong net neutrality provision was one of the issues he specifically singled out for attention. S. 2686 provisions relating to streamlining the video franchising process, universal service fund reform, and net neutrality were the major focus of Commerce Committee hearing held on May 18, and May 25,2006. The Commerce Committee issued a revised draft of the bill which was the subject of a hearing held on June 13, 2006.

After a lengthy and intense markup the Senate Commerce Committee approved (15-7) on June 28, 2006 the newly titled "Advanced Telecommunications and Opportunity Reform Act," which technically is an amended version in the nature of a substitute for H.R. 5252. In addition to a new bill name and number the three-day markup led to the approval of a significant manager's amendment containing a new title and 70 amendments resulting in the passage of a 200-plus page omnibus telecommunications measure. S. 2686, which is now referred to as "the Senate Committee passed version of H.R. 5252," contains 11 titles covering a wide range of telecommunications issues including video franchise reform, net neutrality, universal service reform, municipal broadband, broadcast flag, the digital television transition, interoperability, the illegal transmission of child pornography, and FCC reform. The issue of net neutrality proved to be major point of contention during the markup. Despite the addition of a new title (Title IX) establishing an "Internet Consumer Bill of Rights" net neutrality advocates continued to press for a net neutrality non-discrimination provision. A nondiscrimination amendment offered during markup was defeated by an 11-11 vote, but it is anticipated that proponents of a non-discrimination provision will continue to press the issue if the bill reaches the floor. The lack of a cable franchise build-out provision, federal preemption of state authority over wireless services, as well as provisions added during markup to exempt, for three years, wireless providers from"new and discriminatory" taxes and make permanent the Internet tax moratorium have also resulted in concern.

Both the Senate and House Judiciary Committees have also announced intentions to examine issues related to telecommunications reform. The House Judiciary's Telecommunications and Antitrust Task Force held a hearing on April 25, 2006, to examine competition issues relating to Internet access and "net neutrality." House Judiciary Committee Chairman Sensenbrenner and Representative Conyers, the ranking minority member, stated, in a letter sent to House Speaker Hastert, that the Judiciary Committee has oversight over market conditions, consolidations and antitrust protections in the telecommunications sector, and asked for a sequential referral of H.R. 5252. That request was denied. However, Chairman Sensenbrenner, Representative Conyers and others introduced a bipartisan bill (H.R. 5417) focusing on Internet access from an antitrust perspective, that passed (20-13) the Judiciary Committee, with amendment, on May 25, 2006. A request to the House Rules Committee to have the bill considered as an amendment during floor action on H.R. 5252 was denied. The Senate Judiciary Committee held a June 14, 2006 hearing to examine communications laws in the context of ensuring competition and innovation.

109TH CONGRESS LEGISLATION

H.R. 144 (McHugh)
Rural America Digital Accessibility Act. Provides for grants, loans, research, and tax credits to promote broadband deployment in underserved rural areas. Introduced January 4, 2005; referred to Committee on Energy and Commerce and the Committee on Ways and Means.

H.R. 146 (McHugh)
Establishes a grant program to support broadband-based economic development efforts. Introduced January 4, 2005; referred to Committee on Transportation and Infrastructure and to Committee on Financial Services.

H.R. 214 (Stearns)
Advanced Internet Communications Services Act of 2005. Seeks to promote investment in and deployment of advanced Internet communications services by placing limitations on FCC and state regulation of those services. Introduced January 14, 2005; referred to Committee on Energy and Commerce.

H.R. 1479 (Udall)
Rural Access to Broadband Service Act. Establishes a Rural Broadband Office within the Department of Commerce which would coordinate federal government resources with respect to expansion of broadband services in rural areas. Directs the National Science Foundation to conduct research in enhancing rural broadband. Expresses the Sense of Congress that the broadband loan program in the Rural Utilities Service should be fully funded. Provides for the expensing of broadband Internet access expenditures for rural communities. Introduced April 5, 2005; referred to Committees on Science and on Energy and Commerce.

H.R. 2418 (Gordon)

IP-Enabled Voice Communications and Public Safety Act of 2005. Encourages the rapid deployment of Internet Protocol (IP) enabled voice services for emergency services including 911 and E-911 calls. Introduced May 18, 2005; referred to Committee on Energy and Commerce.

H.R. 2726 (Sessions)

Preserving Innovation in Telecom Act of 2005. Prohibits municipal governments from offering telecommunications, information, or cable services except to remedy market failures by private enterprises to provide such services. Introduced May 26, 2005; referred to Committee on Energy and Commerce.

H.R. 3146 (Blackburn)

Video Choice Act of 2005. Seeks to promote deployment of competitive video services and to eliminate redundant and unnecessary regulation. Introduced June 30, 2005; referred to Committee on Energy and Commerce.

H.R. 3517 (Andrews)

Greater Access to E-Governance Act (GATE Act). Establishes a grant program in the Department of Commerce to provide funds to State and local governments to enable them to deploy broadband computer networks for the conduct of electronic governance transactions by citizens in local schools and libraries. Introduced July 28, 2005; referred to Committee on Energy and Commerce.

H.R. 3958 (Melancon)

Louisiana Katrina Reconstruction Act. Provides grants for construction of broadband infrastructure necessary for technology and economic development in areas affected by Hurricane Katrina. Introduced September 29, 2005; referred to multiple committees.

H.R. 4297 (Thomas)

Tax Relief Act of 2005. Provides a tax credit to holders of rural renaissance bonds funding qualified projects including expanding broadband technology in rural areas. Passed by House December 8, 2005; passed by Senate February 2, 2006.

H.R. 5072 (Terry)

Universal Reform Act of 2006. Targets universal service support specifically to eligible telecommunications carriers in high-cost geographic areas to ensure that communications services and high-speed broadband services are made available throughout all of the States of the United States in a fair and equitable manner. Introduced March 30, 2006; referred to Committee on Energy and Commerce.

H.R. 5252 (Barton)

Communications Opportunity, Promotion, and Enhancement Act of 2006. A bill to promote the deployment of broadband networks and services. Passed House Committee on Energy and Commerce, April 26, 2006; formally introduced May 1, 2006. Reported by the Committee on Energy and Commerce (H.Rept. 109-470), May 17, 2006. Supplemental report filed (H.Rept. 109-470, Part II), June 6, 2006. Passed (321-101) the House, as amended, June 8, 2006.

H.R. 5273 (Markey)

Network Neutrality Act of 2006. A bill to promote open broadband networks and innovation, foster electronic commerce, and safeguard consumer access to online content and services. Introduced May 2, 2006; referred to Committee on Energy and Commerce.

H.R. 5417 (Sensenbrenner)

Internet Freedom and Nondiscrimination Act of 2006. A bill to amend the Clayton Act to ensure competitive and nondiscriminatory access to the Internet. Introduced May 18, 2006; referred to Committee on the Judiciary. Passed (20-13) the full committee, with amendment, May 25, 2006.

H.R. 5970 (Thomas, William)

Estate Tax and Extension of Tax Relief Act of 2006. Provides a tax credit to holders of rural renaissance bonds funding qualified projects including expanding broadband technology in rural areas. Passed House July 29, 2006.

S. 14 (Stabenow)

Fair Wage, Competition, and Investment Act of 2005. Allows the expensing of broadband Internet access expenditures. Introduced January 24, 2005; referred to Committee on Finance.

S. 497 (Salazar)

Broadband Rural Revitalization Act of 2005. Establishes a Rural Broadband Office within the Department of Commerce which would coordinate federal government resources with respect to expansion of broadband services in rural areas. Expresses the Sense of Congress that the broadband loan program in the Rural Utilities Service should be fully funded. Provides for the expensing of broadband Internet access expenditures for rural communities. Introduced March 2, 2005; referred to Committee on Finance.

S. 502 (Coleman)

Rural Renaissance Act. Creates a Rural Renaissance Corporation which would fund qualified projects including projects to expand broadband technology in rural areas. Introduced March 3, 2005; referred to Committee on Finance.

S. 1063 (Nelson)

IP-Enabled Voice Communications and Public Safety Act of 2005. Encourages the rapid deployment of Internet Protocol (IP) enabled voice services for emergency services including 911 and E-911 calls. Introduced May 18, 2005; referred to Committee on Commerce, Science and Transportation.

S. 1147 (Rockefeller)

Amends the Internal Revenue Code of 1986 to provide for the expensing of broadband Internet access expenditures. Introduced May 26, 2005; referred to Committee on Finance.

S. 1294 (Lautenberg)

Community Broadband Act of 2005. Amends the Telecommunications Act of 1996 to preserve and protect the ability of local governments to provide broadband capability and services. Introduced June 23, 2005; referred to Committee on Commerce, Science and Transportation.

S. 1349 (Smith)

Video Choice Act of 2005. Seeks to promote deployment of competitive video services, eliminate redundant and unnecessary regulation, and further the development of next generation broadband networks. Introduced June 30, 2005; referred to Committee on Commerce, Science and Transportation.

S. 1504 (Ensign)

Broadband Investment and Consumer Choice Act. Seeks to establish a market drive telecommunications marketplace, to eliminate government managed competition of existing communication service, and to provide parity between functionally equivalent services. Introduced July 27, 2005; referred to Committee on Commerce, Science and Transportation.

S. 1583 (Smith)

Universal Service for the 21st Century Act. Amends the Communications Act of 1934 to expand the contribution base for universal service and to establish a separate account within the universal service fund to support the deployment of broadband service in unserved areas of the United States. Introduced July 29, 2005; referred to Committee on Commerce, Science and Transportation.

S. 1765 (Landrieu)

Louisiana Katrina Reconstruction Act. Provides grants for construction of broadband infrastructure necessary for technology and economic development in areas affected by Hurricane Katrina. Introduced September 22, 2005; referred to Committee on Finance.

S. 1766 (Vitter)

Louisiana Katrina Reconstruction Act. Provides grants for construction of broadband infrastructure necessary for technology and economic development in areas affected by Hurricane Katrina. Introduced September 22, 2005; referred to Committee on Finance.

S. 1932 (Gregg)

Deficit Reduction Act of 2005. Section 1401 cancels unobligated funds remaining as of October 1, 2006 for the USDA Rural Utilities Service Rural Broadband Access Loan and Loan Guarantee Program. Passed Senate, November 3, 2005. House agreed to conference report (H.Rept. 109-362), December 19, 2005. Senate agreed to conference report with amendments, December 21, 2005. House agreed to amended conference report, February 1, 2006. **P.L. 109-171** signed by President, February 8, 2006.

S. 2020 (Grassley)

Tax Relief Act of 2005. Provides a tax credit to holders of rural renaissance bonds funding qualified projects including expanding broadband technology in rural areas. Passed by Senate as H.R. 4297, February 2, 2006. Provision not retained in Conference Report.

S. 2113 (De Mint)

Digital Age Communications Act of 2005. Promotes the widespread availability of communications services and the integrity of communications facilities, and to encourage investment in communications networks. Introduced December 15, 2005; referred to Committee on Commerce, Science, and Transportation.

S. 2256 (Burns)

Internet and Universal Service Act of 2006. Amends the Communications Act of 1934 to ensure the availability to all Americans of high-quality, advanced telecommunications and broadband services, technologies, and networks at just, reasonable, and affordable rates, and to establish a permanent mechanism to guarantee specific, sufficient, and predictable support for the preservation and advancement of universal service. Introduced February 8, 2006; referred to Committee on Commerce, Science, and Transportation.

S. 2327 (Allen)

Wireless Innovation Act of 2006. Directs the FCC to complete its proceeding on unused broadcast television spectrum ("white space"). Introduced February 17, 2006; referred to Committee on Commerce, Science, and Transportation.

S. 2332 (Stevens)

American Broadband for Communities Act. Makes unused broadcast television spectrum available for wireless broadband. Introduced February 17, 2006; referred to Committee on Commerce, Science, and Transportation.

S. 2357 (Kennedy)

Right TRACK Act. Directs the President's Council of Advisors on Science and Technology to establish a national broadband policy for improving and expanding broadband access in the United States by 2010. Introduced March 2, 2006; referred to Committee on Finance.

S. 2360 (Wyden)

Internet Non-Discrimination Act of 2006. A bill to ensure and promote a free and open Internet for all Americans. Introduced March 2, 2006; referred to Committee on Commerce, Science, and Transportation.

S. 2686 (Stevens)

Communications, Consumer's Choice, and Broadband Deployment Act of 2006. A bill to amend the Communications Act of 1934 and for other purposes. Introduced May 1, 2006; passed (15-7) as amended, the Committee on Commerce, Science, and Transportation, June 28, 2006.

S. 2917 (Snowe)

Internet Freedom Preservation Act. A bill to amend the Communications Act of 1934 to ensure net neutrality. Introduced May 19, 2006; referred to Committee on Commerce, Science, and Transportation.

S. 2989 (Hutchison)

A bill to reform the franchise procedure relating to cable service and video service, and for other purposes. Introduced May 23, 2006; referred to Committee on Commerce, Science, and Transportation.

S. 3820 (Durbin)

Broadband for Rural America Act of 2006. Establishes a Broadband Access Trust Fund and Office of Broadband Access within the FCC to provide grants to study the lack of affordable broadband in unserved areas. Also reforms FCC's broadband data reporting and USDA's broadband loan and grant programs, provides for spectrum auction for wireless rural broadband, and establishes a public-private Rural Broadband Access Task Force. Introduced August 3, 2006; referred to Committee on Commerce, Science, and Transportation.

S. 3829 (Stabenow)

Tax Relief and Minimum Wage Act of 2006. Provides a tax credit to holders of rural renaissance bonds funding qualified projects including expanding broadband technology in rural areas. Introduced August 3, 2006; referred to Committee on Finance.

REFERENCES

[1]   For further information, see CRS Report RS20993, *Wireless Technology and Spectrum Demand: Third Generation (3G) and Beyond*, by Linda K. Moore.

[2]   For further information, see CRS Report RL32421, *Broadband Over Power Lines: Regulatory and Policy Issues*, by Patricia Moloney Figliola.

[3]   FCC, High-Speed Services for Internet Access: Status as of December 31, 2005, July 2006. Available at [http://hraunfoss.fcc.gov/edocs_public/attachmatch/DOC-266596A1.pdf]

[4]   U.S. Government Accountability Office, *Broadband Deployment is Extensive throughout the United States, but It Is Difficult to Assess the Extent of Deployment Gaps in Rural Areas*, GAO-06-426, May 2006, p. 3.

[5]   Federal Communications Commission, Fourth Report to Congress, "*Availability of Advanced Telecommunications Capability in the United States*," GN Docket No. 04-54, FCC 04-208, September 9, 2004, p. 38. Available at [http://hraunfoss.fcc.gov/edocs_public/attachmatch/FCC-04-208A1.pdf]

[6]   International Telecommunications Union, Economies by broadband penetration, 2005. Available at [http://www.itu.int/ITU-D/ict/statistics/at_glance/top20_broad_2005.html]

[7]   OECD, Broadband Access in OECD Countries per 100 inhabitants, December 2005. Available at [http://www.oecd.org/document/39/0,2340,en_2825_ 495656_ 36459431_ 1_1_1_1,00.ht ml#Data2005]

[8]   OECD, Directorate for Science, Technology and Industry, *The Development of Broadband Access in OECD Countries*, October 29, 2001, 63 pages. For a comparison of government broadband policies, also see OECD, Directorate for Science, Technology and Industry, Broadband Infrastructure Deployment: The Role of Government Assistance, May 22, 2002, 42 pages.

[9]   FCC, High-Speed Services for Internet Access: Status as of December 31, 2005, July 2006, p. 4. Available at [http://hraunfoss.fcc.gov/edocs_public/attachmatch/DOC-266596A1.pdf]

[10]   Fourth Report, p. 8.

[11]   See Appendix C of the Fourth Report, *"List of Broadband-Related Proceedings at the Commission,"* pp. 54-56.

[12]   Ibid., p. 9.

[13]   Ibid., p. 5, 7.

[14]   U.S. Government Accountability Office, *Broadband Deployment is Extensive throughout the United States, but It Is Difficult to Assess the Extent of Deployment Gaps in Rural Areas*, GAO-06-426, May 2006, p. 3.

[15]   See speech by Nancy Victory, Assistant Secretary for Communications and Information, before the National Summit on Broadband Deployment, October 25, 2001, [http://www.ntia.doc.gov/ntiahome/speeches/2001/broadband_102501.htm].

[16]   Address by Nancy Victory, NTIA Administrator, before the Alliance for Public Technology Broadband Symposium, February 8, 2002, [http://www.ntia.doc.gov/ntiahome/speeches/2002/apt_020802.htm]

[17]   Allen, Mike, *"Bush Sets Internet Access Goal,"* Washington Post, March 27, 2004.

[18]   See White House, A New Generation of American Innovation, April 2004. Available at [http://www.whitehouse.gov/infocus/technology/economic_policy200404/innovation.pdf]

[19]   Available at [http://www.technology.gov/reports/TechPolicy/Broadband_020921.pdf]

[20]   President's Council of Advisors on Science and Technology, Office of Science and Technology Policy, Building Out Broadband, December 2002, 14 p. Available at [http://www.ostp.gov/PCAST/FINAL%20Broadband%20Report%20With%20Letters.pdf]

[21]   For a discussion on how the broadband provision of P.L. 107-171 has been funded in the 108th and the 109th Congress, see CRS Report RL30719, *Broadband Internet Access and the Digital Divide: Federal Assistance Programs*, by Lennard G. Kruger.

[22]   For further information see CRS Report RL32949, *Communications Act Revisions: Selected Issues for Consideration*, Angele A. Gilroy, coordinator.

[23]   For further information on the net neutrality debate, see CRS Report RS22444, *Net Neutrality: Background and Issues*, by Angele A. Gilroy.

In: Broadband Internet: Access, Regulation and Policy   ISBN: 978-1-60456-073-2
Editor: Ellen S. Cohen, pp. 95-113   © 2007 Nova Science Publishers, Inc.

Chapter 5

BROADBAND LOAN AND GRANT PROGRAMS IN THE USDA'S RURAL UTILITIES SERVICE[*]

Lennard G. Kruger

Science and Technology Resources,
Science, and Industry Division

ABSTRACT

Given the large potential impact broadband access to the Internet may have on the economic development of rural America, concern has been raised over a "digital divide" between rural and urban or suburban areas with respect to broadband deployment. While there are many examples of rural communities with state of the art telecommunications facilities, recent surveys and studies have indicated that, in general, rural areas tend to lag behind urban and suburban areas in broadband deployment.

Citing the lagging deployment of broadband in many rural areas, Congress and the Administration acted in 2001 and 2002 to initiate pilot broadband loan and grant programs within the Rural Utilities Service (RUS) at the U.S. Department of Agriculture (USDA). Subsequently, Section 6103 of the Farm Security and Rural Investment Act of 2002 (P.L. 107-171) amended the Rural Electrification Act of 1936 to authorize a loan and loan guarantee program to provide funds for the costs of the construction, improvement, and acquisition of facilities and equipment for broadband service in eligible rural communities. Currently, RUS/USDA houses the only two federal assistance programs *exclusively* dedicated to financing broadband deployment: the Rural Broadband Access Loan and Loan Guarantee Program and the Community Connect Grant Program.

RUS broadband loan and grant programs have been awarding funds to entities serving rural communities since FY2001. A number of criticisms of the RUS broadband loan and grant programs have emerged, including criticisms related to loan approval and the application process, eligibility criteria, and loans to communities with existing providers.

The current authorization for the Rural Broadband Access Loan and Loan Guarantee Program expires on September 30, 2007. It is expected that the 110th Congress will consider reauthorization of the program as part of the farm bill. Some key issues pertinent

---

[*] Excerpted from CRS Report RL33816, dated February 6, 2007.

to a consideration of the RUS broadband programs include restrictions on applicant eligibility, how "rural" is defined with respect to eligible rural communities, how to address assistance to areas with pre-existing broadband service, technological neutrality, funding levels and mechanisms, and the appropriateness of federal assistance. Ultimately, any modification of rules, regulations, or criteria associated with the RUS broadband program will likely result in "winners and losers" in terms of which companies, communities, regions of the country, and technologies are eligible or more likely to receive broadband loans and grants.

This report will be updated as events warrant.

INTRODUCTION

The Rural Utilities Service (RUS) within the U.S. Department of Agriculture (USDA) houses the only two federal assistance programs *exclusively* dedicated to financing deployment of broadband Internet access in rural America. These are: the Rural Broadband Access Loan and Loan Guarantee Program and the Community Connect Grant Program. The two programs initially appeared as pilot programs in 2001 and 2002. The broadband loan program was authorized by the 2002 farm bill (P.L. 107-171); this authorization expires on September 30, 2007.

The 110th Congress is expected to consider the RUS broadband program as part of the reauthorization of the farm bill in 2007. Given concerns over the lagging status of broadband deployment in many rural areas, Congress is likely to examine how the RUS broadband programs might be positioned to most effectively address rural broadband development. This report provides detailed background information on the RUS broadband loan and grant programs, outlines criticisms of how the RUS broadband program has been implemented thus far, and discusses issues that Congress may be asked to consider during the reauthorization process.

BACKGROUND: BROADBAND AND RURAL AMERICA

The broadband loan and grant programs at RUS are intended to accelerate the deployment of broadband services in rural America. "Broadband" refers to high-speed Internet access for private homes, commercial establishments, schools, and public institutions. Currently in the United States, broadband is primarily provided via cable modem (from the local provider of cable television service) or over the telephone line (digital subscriber line or "DSL"). Other broadband technologies include fiber optic cable, fixed wireless, satellite, and broadband over power lines (BPL).

Broadband access enables a number of beneficial applications to individual users and to communities. These include e-commerce, telecommuting, voice service (voice over the Internet protocol or "VOIP"), distance learning, telemedicine, public safety, and others. It is becoming generally accepted that broadband access in a community can play an important role in economic development. A February 2006 study by the Massachusetts Institute of Technology for the Department of Commerce's Economic Development Administration marked the first attempt to measure the impact of broadband on economic growth. The study found that "between 1998 and 2002, communities in which mass-market broadband was available by December 1999 experienced more rapid growth in employment, the number of businesses overall, and businesses in IT-intensive sectors, relative to comparable communities without broadband at that time."[1]

Access to affordable high-speed Internet service is viewed as particularly important for the economic development of rural areas because it enables individuals and businesses to participate fully in the online economy regardless of geographical location. For example, aside from enabling existing businesses to remain in their rural locations, broadband access could attract new business enterprises drawn by lower costs and a more desirable lifestyle. Essentially, broadband potentially allows businesses and individuals in rural America to live locally while competing globally in an online environment.

Given the large potential impact broadband may have on the economic development of rural America, concern has been raised over a "digital divide" between rural and urban or suburban areas with respect to broadband deployment. While there are many examples of rural communities with state of the art telecommunications facilities,[2] recent surveys and studies have indicated that, in general, rural areas tend to lag behind urban and suburban areas in broadband deployment. For example:

- A September 2004 Department of Commerce report, *A Nation Online: Entering the Broadband Age*, found that a lower percentage of Internet households have broadband in rural areas (24.7%) than in urban areas (40.4%), and that "while broadband usage has grown significantly in all areas since the previous survey, the rural-urban differential continues."[3] The report also found that broadband penetration rates are higher in the West and Northeast than in the South and Midwest.[4]
- December 2005 data from the Pew Internet and American Life Project indicated that while broadband adoption is growing in urban, suburban, and rural areas, broadband users make up larger percentages of urban and suburban users than rural users. Pew found that the percentage of all U.S. adults with broadband at home is 38% for urban areas, 40% for suburban areas, and 24% for rural areas.[5]
- A May 2006 report released by the Government Accountability Office (GAO) found that 17% of rural households subscribe to broadband, as opposed to 28% of suburban and 29% of urban households.[6] GAO also found that lower broadband subscription rates in rural areas are related to availability, not to a lesser tendency of rural households to purchase broadband service.[7]
- Finally, and most recently, in the latest Federal Communications Commission (FCC) data on the deployment of high-speed Internet connections (released January 2007), high-speed subscribers were reported in 99% of the most densely populated zip codes, as opposed to 89% of zip codes with the lowest population densities.[8]

The comparatively lower population density of rural areas is likely the major reason why broadband is less deployed than in more highly populated suburban and urban areas. Particularly for wireline broadband technologies — such as cable modem and DSL — the greater the geographical distances among customers, the larger the cost to serve those customers. For example, in providing telecommunications services, investment per subscriber in rural systems averages $2,921 compared to $1,920 for urban.[9] Thus, there is often less incentive for companies to invest in broadband in rural areas than, for example, in an urban area where there is more demand (more customers with perhaps higher incomes) and less cost to wire the market area.

The terrain of rural areas can also be a hindrance, in that it is more expensive to deploy broadband technologies in a mountainous or heavily forested area. An additional added cost factor for remote areas can be the expense of "backhaul" (e.g. the "middle mile") which refers to the installation of a dedicated line which transmits a signal to and from an Internet backbone which is typically located in or near an urban area.

Cable modem and DSL currently comprise about 90% of broadband deployment nationwide.[10] However, because of the challenges of deploying these technologies in low population density areas, other broadband technologies have been identified as perhaps offering potential in rural areas. These include fixed wireless (WIMAX, wi-fi), satellite, and broadband over powerlines (BPL).

PILOT BROADBAND LOAN AND GRANT PROGRAMS

Given the lagging deployment of broadband in rural areas, Congress and the Administration acted to initiate pilot broadband loan and grant programs within the Rural Utilities Service of the U.S. Department of Agriculture. While RUS had long maintained telecommunications loan and grant programs (Rural Telephone Loans and Loan Guarantees, Rural Telephone Bank, and more recently, the Distance Learning and Telemedicine Loans and Grants) none were exclusively dedicated to financing rural broadband deployment. Title III of the FY2001 agriculture appropriations bill (P.L. 106-387) directed USDA/RUS to conduct a "pilot program to finance broadband transmission and local dial-up Internet service in areas that meet the definition of 'rural area' used for the Distance Learning and Telemedicine Program."

Subsequently, on December 5, 2000, RUS announced the availability of $100 million in loan funding through a one-year pilot program "to finance the construction and installation of broadband telecommunications services in rural America."[11] The broadband pilot loan program was authorized under the authority of the Distance Learning and Telemedicine Program (7 U.S.C. 950aaa), and was available to "legally organized entities" not located within the boundaries of a city or town having a population in excess of 20,000.

The FY2001 pilot broadband loan program received applications requesting a total of $350 million. RUS approved funding for 12 applications totaling $100 million. The FY2002 agriculture appropriations bill (P.L. 107-76) designated a loan level of $80 million for broadband loans, and on January 23, 2002, RUS announced that the pilot program would be extended into FY2002, with $80 million in loans made available to fund many of the applications that did not receive funding during the previous year.[12]

Meanwhile, the FY2002 agriculture appropriations bill (P.L. 107-76) allocated $20 million for a pilot broadband grant program, also authorized under the Distance Learning and Telemedicine Program. On July 8, 2002, RUS announced the availability of $20 million for a pilot grant program for the provision of broadband service in rural America. The program was specifically targeted to economically challenged rural communities with no existing broadband service. Grants were made available to entities providing "community-oriented connectivity" which the RUS defined as those entities "who will connect the critical community facilities including the local schools, libraries, hospitals, police, fire and rescue services and who will operate a community center that provides free and open access to residents."[13]

In response to the July 8, 2002, Notice of Funds Availability, RUS received more than 300 applications totaling more than $185 million in requested grant funding. RUS approved 40 grants totaling $20 million. The pilot program was extended into FY2003, as the Consolidated Appropriations Resolution of 2003 (P.L. 108-7) allocated $10 million for broadband grants. On September 24, 2003, 34 grants were awarded to eligible applicants who did not receive funding during the previous year.

RURAL BROADBAND ACCESS LOAN
AND LOAN GUARANTEE PROGRAM

Building on the pilot broadband loan program at RUS, Section 6103 of the Farm Security and Rural Investment Act of 2002 (P.L. 107-171) amended the Rural Electrification Act of 1936 to authorize a loan and loan guarantee program to provide funds for the costs of the construction, improvement, and acquisition of facilities and equipment for broadband service in eligible rural communities.[14] Section 6103 made available, from the funds of the Commodity Credit Corporation (CCC), a total of $100 million through FY2007 ($20 million for each of fiscal years 2002 through 2005, and $10 million for each of fiscal years 2006 and 2007). P.L. 107-171 also authorized any other funds appropriated for the broadband loan program.

Beginning in FY2004, Congress has annually blocked mandatory funding from the CCC. Thus — starting in FY2004 — the program has been funded as part of annual appropriations in the Distance Learning and Telemedicine account within the Department of Agriculture appropriations bill. Every fiscal year, Congress has approved an appropriation for the loan program which is used to subsidize a specific loan level (the total amount of lending authority). Table 1 shows — for the life of the program to date — loan subsidies, loan levels (lending authority), and actual funds announced by RUS yearly for loan applications. Announced available funding typically exceeds yearly loan levels because large balances of unobligated money have been carried over from year to year. However, Section 1401 of the Deficit Reduction Act of 2005 (P.L. 109-171) cancelled unobligated funds remaining as of October 1, 2006.

For FY2007, the Administration requested a $10.8 million subsidy which would support a loan level of about $357 million ($297 million in Treasury rate loans, $30 million in 4% loans, and $30 million in loan guarantees). The FY2007 House Agriculture Appropriations bill, passed by the House on May 23, 2006 (H.R. 5384; H.Rept. 109-463), would provide $10.8 million (supporting a loan level of $503 million) for the cost of broadband treasury rate loans. On June 22, 2006, the Senate Appropriations Committee approved $10.75 million (S.Rept. 109-266) supporting a Treasury rate loan level of $500 million.

Under the third Continuing Resolution (P.L. 109-383), which provides funding for most federal agencies (including USDA) through February 15, 2007, programs are funded at the lowest of the House, Senate, and FY2006 levels. Under this formula, the broadband loan program is subject to the FY2006 level of $10.75 million for the cost of broadband loans, supporting a loan level of $500 million. H.J.Res. 20, the fourth Continuing Resolution, which would provide funding for the remainder of FY2007, was passed by the House on January 31, 2007. H.J.Res. 20 would fund RUS broadband programs at their FY2006 level.

The President's FY2008 budget proposal was released on February 5, 2007. The Administration requests a $6.45 million (subsidy) to support a loan level of $300 million.

Table 1. Funding for the Rural Broadband Access Loan and Loan Guarantee Program

	Budget Authority (subsidy level)	Loan Level (lending authority)	Announced Available Funding for Loans and Loan Guarantees[a]
FY2003	$40 million[b]	$1.455 billion	$1.455 billion[c]
FY2004	$13.1 million	$602 million	$2.211 billion[d]
FY2005	$11.715 million	$550 million	$2.157 billion[e]
FY2006	$10.75 million	$500 million	$1.085 billion[f]

a. Because all available funds were not awarded, unobligated balances were carried over from year to year.

b. Composed of $20 million from FY2002 plus $20 million for FY2003 of mandatory funding from the Commodity Credit Corporation, as directed by P.L. 107-171. In the FY2004, FY2005, and FY2006 appropriations bills, mandatory funding from the CCC was canceled.

c. Rural Utilities Service, USDA, "Rural Broadband Access Loans and Loan Guarantees Program," *Federal Register*, Vol. 68, No. 20, January 30, 2003, pp. 4753-4755.

d. Rural Utilities Service, USDA, "Rural Broadband Access Loans and Loan Guarantees Program," *Federal Register*, Vol. 69, No.60, March 29, 2004, pp. 16231-16232.

e. Rural Utilities Service, USDA, "Rural Broadband Access Loans and Loan Guarantees Program," *Federal Register*, Vol. 70, No.42, March 4, 2005, pp. 10595-10596.

f. USDA, Rural Utilities Service, "Rural Broadband Access Loan Program," powerpoint presentation, October 19, 2006. Available at [http://www.mnart.org/powerpoint/AnnualMtg /Dominic. ppt#734,13,BroadbandLoan Program:FY2006 Budget].

The Rural Broadband Access Loan and Loan Guarantee Program is codified as 7 U.S.C. 950bb. Specifically, Treasury rate loans, 4% loans, and loan guarantees are authorized for entities providing broadband service for "eligible rural communities," defined as any area of the United States that is not contained in an incorporated city or town with a population in excess of 20,000 inhabitants.[15] RUS is required to be technologically neutral in determining whether or not to make a loan, and is instructed to give priority to rural communities with no existing residential broadband service. Loans are used for financing new or improved existing broadband provider facilities. Loans cannot be used to finance installations or equipment at customers' premises.

On January 30, 2003, the RUS published in the *Federal Register* the regulation (7 CFR part 1738) establishing the Rural Broadband Access Loan and Loan Guarantee Program, as authorized by P.L. 107-171.[16] According to the regulation, entities eligible to receive loans include corporations, limited liability companies, cooperative or mutual organizations, Indian tribes, and public bodies. Specifically **not** eligible are individuals, partnerships, and any entity serving 2% or more of the telephone subscriber lines in the United States. All applicants are required to demonstrate adequate credit support — a minimum of 20% of requested loan amount, including cash on hand equivalent to one full year of operating expense.[17]

To be eligible for 4% loans, applicants must be proposing to serve a community with no existing broadband service, a population of 2,500 or less, and a service area with population density of no more than 20 persons per square mile. Additionally, the community must be located in a county with a per capita income of less than or equal to 65% of the national per capita income.

As of September 30, 2006, the broadband loan program received 185 applications, requesting a total of $3.546 billion in loans. As of September 30, 63 applications were approved (totaling $1.1 billion), 20 were in review (totaling $930 million), and 102 had been returned (totaling $1.516 billion).[18]

Applications for the Rural Broadband Access Loan and Loan Guarantee program are accepted at any time. The maximum loan amount for 4% loans is $7.5 million. There is no maximum for treasury rate loans, and the minimum level for all loans is $100 thousand. Loans are made for the term equal to the expected service life of financed facilities. Further information, including application materials and guidelines, is available at [http://www.usda.gov/rus/telecom/broadband.htm].

COMMUNITY CONNECT BROADBAND GRANTS

The Consolidated Appropriations Act of 2004 (P.L. 108-199) appropriated $9 million "for a grant program to finance broadband transmission in rural areas eligible for Distance Learning and Telemedicine Program benefits authorized by 7 U.S.C. 950aaa." On July 28, 2004, RUS published its final rule on the broadband grant program, called the Community Connect Grant Program (7 CFR part 1739, subpart A).[19] Essentially operating the same as the pilot broadband grants, the program provides grant money to applicants proposing to provide broadband on a "community-oriented connectivity" basis to currently unserved rural areas for the purpose of fostering economic growth and delivering enhanced health care, education, and public safety services.

Funding for the broadband grant program is provided through annual appropriations in the Distance Learning and Telemedicine account within the Department of Agriculture appropriations bill. Table 2 shows a history of appropriations for the Community Connect Broadband Grants (including the pilot grants of FY2002 and FY2003).

For FY2007, the Administration requested zero funding for broadband grants. The FY2007 House Agriculture Appropriations bill, passed by the House on May 23, 2006 (H.R. 5384; H.Rept. 109-463), would provide $8.9 million for broadband grants. On June 22, 2006, the Senate Appropriations Committee approved $10 million for broadband grants (S.Rept. 109-266).

Under the 3rd Continuing Resolution (P.L. 109-383), which provides funding for most federal agencies (including USDA) through February 15, 2007, programs are funded at the lowest of the House, Senate, and FY2006 levels. Under this formula, the broadband grant program is subject to the House level of $8.9 million. H.J.Res. 20, the 4th Continuing Resolution, which would provide funding for the remainder of FY2007, was passed by the House on January 31, 2007. H.J.Res. 20 would fund RUS broadband programs at their FY2006 level.

The President's FY2008 budget proposal was released on February 5, 2007. The FY2008 budget proposal requests no funding for the Community Connect Broadband Grant program.

Table 2. Appropriations for the Community Connect
Broadband Grants, FY2002-FY2006

Fiscal Year	Appropriation
FY2002	$20 million
FY2003	$10 million
FY2004	$9 million
FY2005	$9 million
FY2006	$9 million

Source: Compiled by CRS from appropriations bills.

Eligible applicants for broadband grants include incorporated organizations, Indian tribes or tribal organizations, state or local units of government, cooperatives, private corporations, and limited liability companies organized on a for profit or not-for-profit basis. Individuals or partnerships are not eligible.

Funded projects must: serve a rural area of 20,000 population or less[20] where broadband service does not exist, serve one and only one single community, deploy free basic broadband service (defined as 200 kbps in both directions) for at least two years to all community facilities, offer basic broadband to residential and business customers, and provide a community center with at least ten computer access points within the proposed service area while making broadband available for two years at no charge to users within that community center.

Since the inception of the RUS broadband grant program, $57.7 million in grant money has been awarded to 129 awardees. Awardees must contribute a matching contribution equal to 15% of the requested grant amount.

RUS typically publishes an annual Notice of Funding Availability (NOFA) in the *Federal Register*, which specifies the deadline for applications, the total amount of funding available, and the maximum and minimum amount of funding available for each grant. Further information, including application materials and guidelines, is available at [http://www.usda.gov/rus/telecom/commconnect.htm].

OTHER BROADBAND PROGRAMS

The Rural Broadband Access Loan and Loan Guarantee Program and the Community Connect Broadband Grants are currently the only federal programs *exclusively* dedicated to deploying broadband infrastructure. However, there exist other federal programs that provide financial assistance for various aspects of telecommunications development.[21] Though not explicitly or exclusively devoted to broadband, many of those programs are used to help deploy broadband technologies in rural areas. For example, since 1995, the RUS Rural Telephone Loan and Loan Guarantee program — which has traditionally financed telephone voice service in rural areas under 5,000 inhabitants — has required that all telephone facilities receiving financing must be capable of providing DSL broadband service at a rate of at least 1 megabyte per second.[22] The RUS Distance Learning and Telemedicine grants program is used to support deployment of broadband technologies specifically for telemedicine and distance learning applications. Table 3 shows the number of customers receiving broadband due to USDA financing of telecommunications facilities.

Table 3. Number of Customers Receiving New or Improved Telecommunication Services (Broadband) Through USDA Financing of Telecommunications Facilities (millions)

FY01	FY02	FY03	FY04	FY05	FY06	FY07	FY08
0.315	0.31	0.38	0.37	0.24	0.30	0.25	0.24

Sources: U.S. Dept. of Agriculture, *2006 Performance and Accountability Report*, November 2006, p. 82; U.S. Dept. of Agriculture, *FY2008 Budget Summary and Performance Plan*, p. 44.
Note: Customers are defined as access lines financed by the programs.

The other major vehicle for funding telecommunications development in rural areas is the Universal Service Fund (USF).[23] Subsidies provided by USF's Schools and Libraries Program and Rural Health Care Program are used for a variety of telecommunications services, including broadband access. While the USF's High Cost Program does not *explicitly* fund broadband infrastructure, subsidies are used, in many cases, to upgrade existing telephone networks. Regarding the USF High Cost Program, the Congressional Budget Office has found that "current policy implicitly provides funds for broadband in rural areas," adding that:

> Whether such upgrades are motivated by the intention to provide broadband or better conventional telephone service is not immediately clear. However, the fact that wireline carriers as a whole have been losing subscribers and long-distance revenue over the past half decade suggests that at least part of the new investment in local loops has been made with the expectation of generating revenue from broadband subscriptions.[24]

In addition to federal support for broadband deployment, there are programs and activities ongoing at the state and local level. Surveys, assessments, and reports from the American Electronics Association,[25] Technet,[26] the Alliance for Public Technology,[27] the California Public Utilities Commission,[28] and the AEI-Brookings Joint Center[29] have explored state and local broadband programs. A related issue is the emergence of municipal broadband networks (primarily wireless and fiber based) and the debate over whether such networks constitute unfair competition with the private sector.

CRITICISMS OF RUS BROADBAND PROGRAMS

Broadband loan and grant programs have been awarding funds to entities serving rural communities since FY2001. Since their inception, a number of criticisms of the RUS broadband loan and grant programs have emerged.

Loan Approval and Application Process

Perhaps the major criticism of the broadband loan program is that not enough loans are approved, thereby making it difficult for rural communities to take full advantage of the program. As of September 30, 2006, the broadband loan program had received 185 applications, totaling $3.546 billion in requested loans. Of those applications, 63 have been approved, totaling $1.1 billion; 20 are in review, totaling $930 million, and 102 have been returned, totaling $1.5 billion.[30] According to RUS officials, 28% of available loan money was awarded in 2004, and only 5% of available loan money was awarded in 2005.[31]

The loan application process has been criticized as being overly complex and burdensome, requiring applicants to spend months preparing costly market research and engineering assessments. Many applications are rejected because the applicant's business plan is deemed insufficient to support a commercially viable business. The biggest reason for applications being returned is insufficient credit support, whereby applicants do not have sufficient cash-on-hand (one year's worth is required in most cases). The requirement for cash-on-hand is viewed as particularly onerous for small start up companies, many of whom lack sufficient capital to qualify for the loan. Such companies, critics assert, may be those entities most in need of financial assistance.

In report language to the FY2006 Department of Agriculture Appropriations Act (P.L. 109-97), the Senate Appropriations Committee (S.Rept. 109-92) directed the RUS "to reduce the burdensome application process and make the program requirements more reasonable, particularly in regard to cash-on-hand requirements." The Committee also directed USDA to hire more full-time employees to remedy delays in application processing times.

At a May 17, 2006 hearing held by the Senate Committee on Agriculture, Nutrition, and Forestry, the Administrator of the RUS stated that RUS is working to make the program more user friendly, while at the same time protecting taxpayer investment:

> As good stewards of the taxpayers' money, we must make loans that are likely to be repaid. One of the challenges in determining whether a proposed project has a reasonable chance of success is validating the market analysis of the proposed service territory and ensuring that sufficient resources are available to cover operating expenses throughout the construction period until such a time that cash flow from operations become sufficient. The loan application process that we have developed ensures that the applicant addresses these areas and that appropriate resources are available for maintaining a viable operation.[32]

According to RUS, the loan program was initially overwhelmed by applications (particularly during a two week period in August 2003), and as the program matures, application review times have dropped. As of January 2007, there were 21 applications pending requesting a total of $357.165 million.[33]

Eligibility Criteria

Since the inception of the broadband grant and loan programs, the criteria for applicant eligibility has been criticized both for being too broad and for being too narrow. An audit report released by USDA's Office of Inspector General (IG) found that the "programs' focus has shifted away from those rural communities that would not, without Government assistance, have access to broadband technologies."[34] Specifically the IG report found that the RUS definition of rural area has been "too broad to distinguish usefully between suburban and rural communities,"[35] with the result that, as of March 10, 2005, $103.4 million in loans and grants (nearly 12% of total funding awarded) had been awarded to 64 communities located near large cities. The report cited examples of affluent suburban subdivisions qualifying as rural areas under the program guidelines and receiving broadband loans.[36]

On the other hand, eligibility requirements have also been criticized as too narrow. For example, the limitation of assistance only to communities of 20,000 or less in population excludes small rural towns that may exceed this limit, and also excludes many municipalities seeking to deploy their own networks.[37] Similarly, per capita income requirements can preclude higher income communities with higher costs of living (e.g. rural Alaska), and the limitation of grant programs only to underserved areas excludes rural communities with existing but very limited broadband access.[38]

Loans to Communities with Existing Providers

The USDA Rural Broadband Access statute (7 U.S.C. 950bb) specifies that the program "shall give priority to eligible rural communities in which broadband service is not available to residential customers." The IG report found that RUS too often has given loans to communities with existing broadband service. The IG report found that "RUS has not ensured that communities without broadband service receive first priority for loans," and that although RUS has a system in place to prioritize loans to unserved communities, the system "lacks a cutoff date and functions as a rolling selection process — priorities are decided based on the applicants who happen to be in the pool at any given moment."[39] The result is that a significant number of communities with some level of preexisting broadband service have received loans. According to the IG report, of 11 loans awarded in 2004, 66% of the associated communities served by those loans had existing service. According to RUS, 31% of communities served by all loans (during the period 2003 through early 2005) had preexisting competitive service (not including loans used to upgrade or expand existing service).[40] In some cases, according to the IG report, "loans were issued to companies in highly competitive business environments where multiple providers competed for relatively few customers."[41]

Awarding loans to entities in communities with preexisting competitive service has raised criticism from competitors who already offer broadband to those communities. According to the National Cable and Telecommunications Association (NCTA), "RUS loans are being used to unfairly subsidize second and third broadband providers in communities where private risk capital already has been invested to provide broadband service."[42] Critics argue that providing loans in areas with preexisting competitive broadband service creates an uneven playing field and discourages further private investment in rural broadband.[43] In response, RUS stated in the IG report that its policies are in accordance with the statute, and that they address "the need for competition to increase the quality of services and reduce the cost of those services to the consumer."[44] RUS argues that the presence of a competitor does not necessarily mean that an area is adequately served, and additionally, that in order for some borrowers to maintain a viable business in an unserved area, it may be necessary for that company to also be serving more densely populated rural areas where some level of competition already exists.[45]

ISSUES FOR REAUTHORIZATION

The current authorization for the Rural Broadband Access Loan and Loan Guarantee program expires on September 30, 2007. It is expected that the 110th Congress will consider reauthorization of the program as part of a possible 2007 farm bill. Any modification of rules, regulations, or criteria associated with the RUS broadband program will likely result in "winners and losers" in terms of which companies, communities, regions of the country, and technologies are eligible or more likely to receive broadband loans and grants. The following are some key issues pertinent to a consideration of the RUS broadband programs.

Restricting Applicant Eligibility

The RUS broadband program has been criticized for excluding too many applicants due to stringent financial requirements (e.g. the requirement that an applicant have a year's worth of cash-on-hand) and an application process — requiring detailed business plans and market surveys — that some view as overly expensive and burdensome to complete. During the reauthorization process, Congress may wish to consider whether the criteria for loan eligibility should be modified, and whether a more appropriate balance can be found between the need to make the program more accessible to unserved and often lower-income rural areas, and the need to protect taxpayers against bad loans.

Definition of "Rural Community"

The definition of which communities qualify as "rural" has been changed twice by statute since the broadband loan program was initiated. Under the pilot program, funds were authorized under the Distance Learning and Telemedicine Program, which defines "exceptionally rural areas" (under 5,000 inhabitants), "rural areas" (between 5,000 and 10,000) and "mid-rural areas" (between 10,000 and 20,000). RUS determined that communities of 20,000 or less would be eligible for broadband loans in cases where broadband services did not already exist.

In 2002, this definition was made narrower by the Farm Security and Rural Investment Act (P.L. 107-171), which designated eligible communities as any incorporated or unincorporated place with fewer than 20,000 inhabitants, and which was outside any standard metropolitan statistical area (MSA). The requirement that communities not be located within MSA's effectively prohibited suburban communities from receiving broadband loans. However, in 2004, the definition was again changed by the FY2004 Consolidated Appropriations Act (P.L. 108-199). The act broadened the definition, keeping the population limit at 20,000, but eliminating the MSA prohibition, thereby permitting rural communities near large cities to receive loans. Thus the current definition used for rural communities is the same as what was used for the broadband pilot program, except that loans can now be issued to communities with preexisting service.

The definition of what constitutes a "rural" community is always a difficult issue for Congressional policymakers in determining how to target rural communities for broadband assistance. On the one hand, the narrower the definition the greater the possibility that deserving communities may be excluded. On the other hand, the broader the definition used, the greater the possibility that communities not traditionally considered "rural" or "underserved" may be eligible for financial assistance.

A related issue is the scope of coverage proposed by individual applications. While many of the loan applications propose broadband projects offering service to multiple rural communities, RUS sees a coming trend towards larger regional and national proposals, covering hundreds or even more than a thousand communities.[46] The larger the scope of coverage, the greater the complexity of the loan application and the larger the possible benefits and risks to taxpayers.

Pre-Existing Broadband Service

While the majority of broadband loans (and all broadband grants) are awarded to entities serving areas without pre-existing broadband service, and while RUS is directed by statute to "give priority to eligible rural communities in which broadband service is not available to residential customers," a significant number of Treasury-rate loans have been awarded in areas with pre-existing service. Loans to areas with competitive pre-existing service — that is, areas where existing companies already provide some level of broadband — have sparked controversy because loan recipients are likely to compete with other companies already providing broadband service.

During reauthorization, Congress may be asked to more sharply define whether and/or how loans should be given to companies serving rural areas with preexisting competitive service.[47] On the one hand, one could argue that the federal government should not be subsidizing competitors for broadband service, particularly in sparsely populated rural markets which may be able only to support one provider. Furthermore, keeping communities with preexisting broadband service eligible may divert assistance from unserved areas that are most in need. On other hand, many suburban and urban areas currently receive the benefits of competition between broadband providers —competition which can potentially drive down prices while improving service and performance. It is therefore appropriate, it is argued, that rural areas also receive the benefits of competition, which in some areas may not be possible without federal financial assistance.

Technological Neutrality

The 2002 farm bill (P.L. 107-171) directed RUS to use criteria that are "technologically neutral" in determining which projects to approve for loans. In other words, RUS is prohibited from typically valuing one broadband technology over another when assessing loan applications. As of September 2006, 30% of approved and funded projects employed fiber-to-the-home technology, 24% employed DSL, 22% wireless (unlicensed), 19% hybrid fiber-coaxial (cable), 3% wireless (licensed), and 2% broadband over powerlines (BPL).[48] No funding has been provided for projects utilizing satellite broadband.[49]

While decisions on funded projects are required to be technologically neutral, RUS (through the Secretary of Agriculture) does have the latitude to determine minimum required data transmission rates for broadband projects eligible for funding. According to the statute, "the Secretary shall, from time to time as advances in technology warrant, review and recommend modifications of rate-of-data transmission criteria for purposes of the identification of broadband service technologies." To date, RUS broadband loan and grant programs have required a minimum threshold of 200 kbps (kilobytes per second) in both directions (both uploading and downloading). While the 200 kbps minimum matches the standard definition of broadband that is used by the Federal Communications Commission (FCC), it is considered a low threshold that captures almost all existing broadband technology.[50]

Some have argued that the minimum threshold of 200 kbps should be raised to ensure that rural areas receive "next-generation" broadband technologies with faster data rates capable of more varied and sophisticated applications. On the other hand, significantly raising minimum data rates could exclude certain technologies — for example typical data transmission rates for fiber and some wireless technologies exceed what is offered by "current generation" technologies such as DSL and cable. Proponents of keeping the minimum threshold at a low level could argue that underserved rural areas are best served by any broadband technology that is economically feasible to deploy, regardless of whether it is "next" or "current" generation.

Funding

Under the 2002 farm bill (P.L. 107-171), broadband loan subsidies were funded at a total of $100 million through FY2007 ($20 million for each of fiscal years 2002 through 2005, and $10 million for each of fiscal years 2006 and 2007). This $100 million was to be transferred from funds of the Commodity Credit Corporation (CCC). However, beginning in FY2004, Congress has annually blocked mandatory funding from the CCC, thus ensuring that the program was funded solely through annual appropriations.

During reauthorization, the 110th Congress may wish to consider whether the mandatory CCC funding mechanism provided in the 2002 farm bill should be retained, eliminated, or modified. Also at issue is whether the current funding levels for the RUS broadband programs are optimal. Given the relatively low utilization of the broadband loan program, should funding remain at current levels or below, or alternatively, if modifications are made to ensure fuller utilization, and given the need to bridge the digital divide, should funding be increased? A related issue is whether more money should be shifted from the broadband loan program to the Community Connect broadband grant program, in order to better address the need for broadband in lower income rural communities that may not be able to meet financial criteria necessary to qualify for loans.

Appropriateness of Federal Assistance

Finally, there is the broader issue of whether government intervention in the broadband marketplace is appropriate or effective. Some argue that federal investment in broadband deployment could distort private sector investment decisions in a dynamic and rapidly evolving marketplace,[51] and question whether other strategies — such as deregulation, tax incentives, or spectrum policy — may be more effective in fostering increased broadband deployment.

On the other hand, proponents of financial assistance counter that the available data show, in general, that the private sector will invest in areas where it expects the greatest return — areas of high population density and income. Without some governmental assistance in underserved areas, they argue, it is reasonable to conclude that broadband deployment will lag behind in many rural and low income areas.[52]

ACTIVITIES IN THE 110TH CONGRESS

On January 31, 2007, Secretary of Agriculture Mike Johanns released the Administration's 2007 farm bill proposal. The Administration proposal would reauthorize the Rural Broadband Access Loan and Loan Guarantee program and would allocate $500 million in mandatory spending to reduce the backlog in a number of Rural Development loan and grant programs, including the broadband loan program.

The President's FY2008 budget proposal was released on February 5, 2007. The Administration requests a $6.45 million (subsidy) to support a loan level of $300 million. Noting that this is a $200 million reduction from the FY2007 level, the budget documents state that the "funding is sufficient to meet expected demand," and that:

> Regulations are being changed to correct certain weaknesses that have become apparent since the program was established a few years ago. The new regulations will ensure that program funds are focused on rural areas that are lacking existing providers, and that applicants meet high enough standards to ensure long term success.[53]

The FY2008 budget proposal requests no funding for the Community Connect Broadband Grant program.

REFERENCES

[1]   Gillett, Sharon E., Massachusetts Institute of Technology, *Measuring Broadband's Economic Impact*, report prepared for the Economic Development Administration, U.S. Department of Commerce, February 28, 2006 p. 4. Available at [http://www.eda .gov/ImageCache/EDAPublic/documents/pdfdocs2006/mitcmubbimpactreport_2epdf/v 1/ mitcmubbimpactreport.pdf].

[2]   See for example: National Exchange Carrier Association (NECA), *Trends 2006: Making Progress With Broadband*, 2006, 26 p. Available at [http://www.neca.org/ media/trends_brochure_website.pdf].

[3]   U.S. Department of Commerce, Economics and Statistics Administration, National Telecommunications and Information Administration, *A Nation Online: Entering the Broadband Age*, September 2004, pp. 12-13.

[4]   Ibid., p. 12.

[5]   Horrigan, John B., Pew Internet and American Life Project, *Rural Broadband Internet Use*, February 2006, Available at [http://www.pewinternet.org/ pdfs/ PIP_ Rural_Broadband.pdf].

[6]   U.S. Government Accountability Office, Broadband Deployment is Extensive throughout the United States, but It Is Difficult to Assess the Extent of Deployment Gaps in Rural Areas, GAO-06-426, May 2006, p. 12. Available at [http://www.gao.gov/new.items/d06426.pdf].

[7]   Ibid., p. 5.

[8]   FCC, *High-Speed Services for Internet Access: Status as of June 30, 2006,* January 2007, p. 4. Available at [http://hraunfoss.fcc.gov/edocs_public/attachmatch/DOC-270128A1.pdf].

[9]   Office of Management and Budget, Program Assessment Rating Tool (PART), "Detailed Information on the Rural Telecommunications Loan Programs Assessment," assessment year 2004, available at [http://www.whitehouse.gov/omb/expectmore /detail.10001017.2005.html]

[10] High-Speed Services for Internet Access: Status as of December 31, 2005, Chart 2.

[11] Rural Utilities Service, USDA, "Construction and Installation of Broadband Telecommunications Services in Rural America; Availability of Loan Funds," *Federal Register*, Vol. 65, No. 234, December 5, 2000, p. 75920.

[12] Rural Utilities Service, USDA, "Broadband Pilot Loan Program," *Federal Register*, Vol. 67, No. 15, January 23, 2002, p. 3140.

[13] Rural Utilities Service, USDA, "Broadband Pilot Grant Program," *Federal Register*, Vol. 67, No. 130, July 8, 2002, p. 45080.

[14] Title VI of the Rural Electrification Act of 1936 (7 U.S.C. 950bb).

[15] Section 772 of the FY2004 Consolidated Appropriations Act (P.L. 108-199) changed the definition of an "eligible rural community" to be defined as "any area of the United States that is not contained in an incorporated city or town with a population in excess of 20,000 inhabitants." Accordingly, the March 29, 2004 Notice of Funds Availability for the Rural Broadband Access Loans and Loan Guarantee Program defined "Eligible Rural Community" as follows: The definition of eligible rural community in Section 601(b)(2) of the Rural Electrification Act (7 U.S.C. 950bb)(b)(2), qualifying for financial assistance under the Rural Broadband Access Loan and Loan Guaranty Program, has been amended by provisions in the Consolidated Appropriations Act, 2004, to mean any area of the United States that is not contained in an incorporated city or town with a population in excess of 20,000 inhabitants. Therefore, an applicant no longer must demonstrate that it is not located in an area designated as a standard metropolitan statistical area. This change supersedes and nullifies contrary provisions in regulations implementing the broadband program found at 7 CFR part 1738.

[16] Rural Utilities Service, USDA, "Rural Broadband Access Loans and Loan Guarantees," *Federal Register*, Vol. 68, No. 20, January 30, 2003, pp. 4684-4692.

[17] The cash-on-hand requirement is waived for companies with two previous years of positive cash flow.

[18] A listing of approved and pending applications is available at [http://www.usda.gov/rus/telecom/broadband.htm].

[19] Rural Utilities Service, USDA, "Broadband Grant Program," 7 CFR part 1739, *Federal Register*, Vol. 69, No. 144, July 28, 2004, pp. 44896-44903.

[20] A rural area is defined as "any area of the United States not included within the boundaries of any incorporated or unincorporated city, village, or borough having a population in excess of 20,000 inhabitants." (7 CFR 1739.3)

[21] See CRS Report RL30719, Broadband Internet Access and the Digital Divide: Federal Assistance Programs, by Lennard G. Kruger and Angele A. Gilroy.

[22] In the Rural Electrification Loan Restructuring Act (the 1993 farm bill), Congress amended the Rural Electrification Act to require that facilities financed under this program be capable of providing broadband service at the rate of 1 megabyte per second.

[23] For more information on the Universal Service Fund, see CRS Report RL30719, *Broadband Internet Access and the Digital Divide: Federal Assistance Programs, by* Lennard G. Kruger and Angele A. Gilroy.

[24] Congressional Budget Office, *Factors That May Increase Future Spending from the Universal Service Fund*, CBO Paper, June 2006, p. 25. Available at [http://www.cbo.gov/ftpdocs/72xx/doc7291/06-16-UniversalService.pdf].

[25] American Electronics Association, *Broadband in the States 2003: A State-by-State Overview of Broadband Deployment*, May 22, 2003. Available at [http://www.aeanet.org/publications/idet_broadbandstates03.asp].

[26] TechNet, *The State Broadband Index: An Assessment of State Policies Impacting Broadband Deployment and Demand*, July 17, 2003, 48 p. Available at [http://www.michigan.gov/documents/State_Broadband_Index_71282_7.pdf].

[27] Alliance for Public Technology, *A Nation of Laboratories: Broadband Policy Experiments in the States*, March 5, 2004, 48 p. Available at [http://www.apt.org/publications/reports-studies/broadbandreport_final.pdf].

[28] California Public Utilities Commission, *Broadband Deployment in California*, May 5, 2005, 83 p. Available at [http://www.cpuc.ca.gov/static/ telco/reports/ broadbandreport.htm].

[29] Wallsten, Scott, AEI-Brookings Joint Center for Regulatory Studies, *Broadband Penetration: An Empirical Analysis of State and Federal Policies*, Working Paper 05-12, June 2005, 29 p. Available at [http://aei-brookings.org/admin /authorpdfs/page.php?id=1161].

[30] U.S. Department of Agriculture, Rural Development, "Telecommunications Funding Opportunities," powerpoint presentation, 2006.

[31] GAO, Broadband Deployment is Extensive throughout the United States, but It Is Difficult to Assess the Extent of Deployment Gaps in Rural Areas, p. 33.

[32] Testimony of Jim Andrew, Administrator, Rural Utilities Service, U.S. Department of Agriculture, "Broadband Program Administered by USDA's Rural Utilities Service," full committee hearing before the Senate Committee on Agriculture, Nutrition, and Forestry, 109th Congress, May 17, 2006.

[33] Rural Utilities Service, private communication, January 18, 2007.

[34] U.S. Department of Agriculture, Office of Inspector General, Southwest Region, *Audit Report: Rural Utilities Service Broadband Grant and Loan Programs*, Audit Report

09601-4-Te, September 2005, p. I. Available at [http://www.usda.gov /oig/ webdocs/ 09601-04-TE.pdf].

[35] Ibid., p. 6.

[36] Ibid., p. 8.

[37] Martinez, Michael, "Broadband: Loan Fund's Strict Rules Foil Small Municipalities," *National Journal's Technology Daily*, August 23, 2005.

[38] GAO, Broadband Deployment is Extensive throughout the United States, but It Is Difficult to Assess the Extent of Deployment Gaps in Rural Areas, p. 33-34.

[39] Ibid., p. 13.

[40] Ibid., p. 14.

[41] Ibid., p. 15

[42] Letter from Kyle McSlarrow, President and CEO, National Cable and Telecommunications Association to the Honorable Mike Johanns, Secretary of the U.S. Department of Agriculture, May 16, 2006.

[43] Testimony of Tom Simmons, Vice President for Public Policy, Midcontinent Communications, before Senate Committee on Agriculture, Nutrition, and Forestry, May 17, 2006.

[44] Audit Report: Rural Utilities Service Broadband Grant and Loan Programs, p. 17.

[45] Rural Utilities Service, private communication, January 18, 2007.

[46] Rural Utilities Service, private communication, January 18, 2007.

[47] The statute (7 U.S.C. 950bb) allows States and local governments to be eligible for loans only if "no other eligible entity is already offering, or has committed to offer, broadband services to the eligible rural community."

[48] USDA, Rural Utilities Service, "Rural Broadband Access Loan Program," powerpoint presentation, October 19, 2006.

[49] According to the GAO, satellite companies state that RUS's broadband loan program requirements "are not readily compatible with their business model or technology," and that "because the agency requires collateral for loans, the program is more suited for situations where the providers, rather than individual consumers, own the equipment being purchased through the loan. Yet, when consumers purchase satellite broadband, it is common for them to purchase the equipment needed to receive the satellite signal, such as the reception dish." Satellite companies argue that in some rural areas, satellite broadband might be the most feasible and cost-effective solution. See GAO, *Broadband Deployment is Extensive throughout the United States, but It Is Difficult to Assess the Extent of Deployment Gaps in Rural Areas*, pp. 34-35.

[50] Critics of the FCC's broadband definition of 200 kbps have pointed to higher download and upload speeds typically offered in other countries. See Turner, Derek S., Free Press, *Broadband Reality Check II: The Truth Behind America's Digital Divide*, August 2006, pp 5-9. Available at [http://www.freepress.net/docs/bbrc2-final.pdf]. For further discussion of international broadband speeds and prices, including the differences between advertised and actual speeds, see Kende, Michael, Analysis Consulting Limited, *Survey of International Broadband Offerings*, October 4, 2006, 12 p. Available at [http://www.analysys.com/pdfs/BroadbandPerformanceSurvey.pdf].

[51] See Leighton, Wayne A., *Broadband Deployment and the Digital Divide: A Primer*, a Cato Institute Policy Analysis, No. 410, August 7, 2001, 34 pp. Available at [http://www.cato.org/pubs/pas/pa410.pdf].

[52] See for example: Cooper, Mark, Consumer Federation of America and Consumers Union, *Expanding the Digital Divide and Falling Behind on Broadband*, October 2004, 33 pages. Available at [http://www.consumersunion.org/pub/ddnewbook.pdf].

[53] U.S. Dept. of Agriculture, FY2008 Budget Summary and Performance Plan, p. 44.

In: Broadband Internet: Access, Regulation and Policy   ISBN: 978-1-60456-073-2
Editor: Ellen S. Cohen, pp. 115-131   © 2007 Nova Science Publishers, Inc.

Chapter 6

BROADBAND OVER POWERLINES: REGULATORY AND POLICY ISSUES*

Patricia Moloney Figliola
Telecommunications and Internet Policy Resources,
Science, and Industry Division

ABSTRACT

Congress has expressed significant interest in increasing the availability of broadband services throughout the nation, both in expanding the geographic availability of such services, as well as expanding the service choices available to consumers. Broadband over Powerlines (BPL) has the potential to play a significant role in increasing the competitive landscape of the communications industry but also has the potential to extend the reach of broadband to a greater number of Americans. BPL, like any technology, has its advantages and disadvantages. Proponents state that (1) BPL is less expensive to deploy than the cable and telephone companies' broadband offerings, (2) it does not require upgrades to the actual electric grid, and (3) it is not limited by certain technical constraints of its competitors. However, critics have expressed ongoing concern that BPL could interfere with licensed radio spectrum such as amateur radio, government, and emergency response frequencies.

The Federal Communications Commission (FCC) began investigating BPL in 2003 and adopted a Report and Order (FCC 04-245) in its proceeding in October 2004. Among other items, the Order

- set forth rules imposing new technical requirements on BPL devices;
- established bands within which BPL must avoid operating entirely and "exclusion zones" within which BPL must avoid operating on certain frequencies;
- established a publicly available BPL notification database to facilitate resolution of harmful interference; and
- improved measurement procedures for all equipment that use RF energy to communicate over power lines.

---

* Excerpted from CRS Report RL32421, dated August 4, 2006.

Other FCC proceedings are also related to BPL development, deployment, and regulation. For instance, the Commission ruled on August 5, 2005, that providers of certain voice over Internet Protocol (VoIP) services — such as BPL providers —would be required to accommodate law enforcement wiretaps.

On April 21, 2005, Representative Mike Ross introduced H.Res. 230, to express the sense that the FCC should reconsider and revise its rules governing BPL. The resolution was referred to the Committee on Energy and Commerce Subcommittee on Telecommunications and the Internet on May 13, 2005. Additionally, on April 26, 2006, Mr. Ross introduced an amendment (#25) in committee to the Communications Opportunity, Promotion, and Enhancement Act of 2006 (H.R. 5252) that would require the FCC to study and report on the interference potential of BPL systems within 90 days of the bill's enactment. The amendment passed on a voice vote.

On August 3, 2006, the FCC adopted a Memorandum Opinion and Order acknowledging the significant benefits of BPL, reaffirming its commitment to address interference issues, and reemphasizing that the Part 15 rule changes were made to ensure that BPL operations do not become a source of interference to licensed radio services.

BACKGROUND

Congress has expressed significant, ongoing interest in increasing the availability of broadband[1] services throughout the nation, both in expanding the geographic availability of such services (e.g., into rural as well as more urban areas), as well as expanding the service choices available to consumers (e.g, promoting additional service options at reasonable prices).

The telephone, cable, and satellite industries, and more recently the electric utilities, all provide broadband services to consumers. Electric utilities have long had the ability to send communications over their powerlines through what is called powerline communications (PLC) technology, but that capability was used primarily to maintain the operability of the power grid — remote monitoring of the grid and other management functions. It was not offered as a commercial product because of technical limitations and regulatory limitations under the Public Utility Holding Company Act of 1935 (PUHCA).[2] Specifically, regarding regulatory limitations, PUHCA prohibited electric utilities from entering the retail telecommunications market without all of their operations, including the telecommunications component, being regulated by the Securities and Exchange Commission under PUHCA. However, in 1996, driven by the elimination under the Telecommunications Act of the PUHCA limitations[3] and the increasing demand for broadband services, electric utilities began exploring ways to turn PLC into a commercially viable, consumer service — Broadband over Powerlines (BPL).[4]

Many electric companies are now in the process of upgrading their transmission and distribution systems to provide BPL.[5] This technology has the potential to play a significant role in increasing the competitive landscape of the electric utility and telecommunications industry, as well as making broadband available to more Americans than ever before. BPL, however, like any technology, has its advantages and disadvantages. For example, BPL, in general, is less expensive to deploy than the cable and telephone companies' broadband offerings because it does not require upgrades to the actual electric grid and is not limited by certain technical constraints of its competitors. Specifically, the telephone companies' broadband service, digital subscriber line (DSL), is limited to consumers within 18,000 feet of a central office unless expensive remote equipment is placed close to the customer. Cable companies, while not limited by the same distance restrictions as the telephone companies, still must upgrade their cable plant as well as the equipment at their "head end"[6] to provide cable modem service. Finally, Internet service delivered via satellite is still primarily a downstream-only service, with a dial-up connection required to send data to the Internet. However, critics of BPL have expressed concern that it will interfere with licensed radio spectrum such as amateur radio, government, and emergency response frequencies.

Companies both in the United States and abroad have pilot tested BPL and many are now deploying it commercially. For example, in 2004, Manassas, VA, began testing BPL service and became the first U.S. community with a commercial BPL offering.[7] The service is now being used by roughly 700 of the 12,500 households in the Manassas area with another 500 having requested service. However, in Manassas as well as in other areas where BPL is being deployed, there have been some concerns and difficulties. For example, amateur radio operators have stated their concern that BPL will interfere with their radio signals.[8] Efforts are being made by industry and government to address these concerns while still continuing BPL deployment.

In addition to providing new choices for consumers and increased competition in the broadband market, BPL can provide other benefits, both to the electric utilities and to others. As tests and commercial deployments continue, the electric utilities can capitalize on their existing relationships with consumers and the ubiquity of their networks. Also, BPL can be sold either as a retail service under the electric utility's brand or as a wholesale service to third-party ISPs, offering smaller broadband providers another wire to the customer — and electric utilities have expressed interest in providing such open access on a wholesale basis.[9]

Concerns among electric utilities and investors about BPL deployment do remain, however. Although the pilot tests and limited commercial deployments hace thus far proven successful, the viability of large-scale commercial implementation remains unproven. Also, while name recognition will help the electric utilities as they roll out their service, there is also concern that they may have an unfair competitive advantage over smaller, less established providers. In this case, however, this may not be a significant concern because of the size of the established broadband providers, the telephone and cable companies.[10] Finally, although BPL is likely to be deployed further out into rural areas than either cable or DSL, it remains to be seen if BPL is as economical to deploy in those areas as policymakers and rural consumers hope.

The FCC opened a rulemaking proceeding on the technical issues related to BPL deployment in February 2004 and adopted a Report and Order on the proceeding in October 2004 (ET Docket 04-37, FCC 04-245)[11] (see "Regulatory Activity —Federal Communications Commission," page 6). Congress may wish to monitor how the FCC implements the rules that will guide BPL development and deployment, as well as monitor more general issues surrounding BPL, such as industry and societal issues, regulatory and industry governance issues, and technical issues. These three categories of issues are discussed in detail at the end of this report (see "Issues for Congress").

STAKEHOLDERS

In addition to marketplace competitors and consumers, the key stakeholders in this issue are the BPL industry, amateur radio operators (represented primarily by the American Radio Relay League (ARRL)), and various government entities.

In favor of BPL deployment and the FCC's rules is the BPL industry: the electric power companies, Internet service providers (ISP), BPL equipment manufacturers, BPL system solutions companies (such as Main.net), and the trade associations representing those companies. Trade associations involved include the Edison Electric Institute, the Powerline Communications Association (PLCA), the PLC Forum, United Power Line Council (UPLC), and the United Telecom Council (UTC).[12] These groups have a financial stake in bringing BPL successfully to market and are eager to enter the broadband business.

Amateur radio users have expressed opposition to BPL deployment because of concerns over its potential negative impact — specifically, interference — on amateur radio frequencies by BPL emissions. Although some of its concerns had been addressed in the BPL Report and Order, the ARRL remained concerned about the impact of widespread deployment of these systems.[13]

In addition to the abovementioned groups, several government entities have an interest in how BPL is deployed. Specifically, local and regional emergency responders, the Department of Defense, the Federal Emergency Management Agency (now part of the Department of Homeland Security), and the National Telecommunications and Information Administration (NTIA) within the Department of Commerce have expressed both concern and support for BPL. Although these groups express concerns similar to those of ARRL — namely that BPL could potentially interfere with emergency communications and steps need to be taken to ensure noninterference — they also express support for BPL because they believe it will contribute to a more secure and better-managed electric transmission and distribution network.[14] The NTIA expresses support for BPL because of its potential to further close the "digital divide,"[15] one of its major goals. Further, because of the services that can be offered over BPL (e.g., voice over Internet Protocol [VoIP]), the law enforcement community is also concerned about the regulatory treatment of BPL — specifically, whether BPL services should be subject to federal wiretap requirements set forth in the Communications Assistance for Law Enforcement Act (CALEA).

The FCC has the largest role in how BPL will be deployed. It not only is the regulatory agency that developed the rules governing BPL, it also has a statutory obligation under Section 706 of the Telecommunications Act of 1996 to "encourage the deployment on a reasonable and timely basis of advanced telecommunications capability to all Americans."[16] The FCC, therefore, will maintain a significant influence on how the market for BPL service develops.

FEDERAL COMMUNICATIONS COMMISSION ACTIVITY

The FCC has been investigating BPL since 2003 and adopted rules regulating BPL systems in October 2004; it is also addressing BPL-related issues in its CALEA and IP-Enabled Services Proceedings.

Broadband over Powerline Systems Proceeding

In April 2003, the FCC issued a Notice of Inquiry (NOI),[17] *Inquiry Regarding Carrier Current Systems, including Broadband over Powerline Systems*,[18] to gather comments concerning whether it should amend its Part 15 Rules[19] "to facilitate the deployment of Access BPL while ensuring that licensed services continue to be protected."[20] The FCC received over five thousand initial and reply comments in response to its NOI during July and August 2003. These comments were discussed at length in the FCC's February 2004 Notice of Proposed Rulemaking (NPRM), *Carrier Current Systems, including Broadband over Power Line Systems and Amendment of Part 15 Regarding New Requirements and Measurement Guidelines for Access Broadband over Power Line Systems*.[21] The FCC adopted its Report and Order in this proceeding in October 2004. Specifically, the Order

- set forth rules imposing new technical requirements on BPL devices, such as the capability to avoid using any specific frequency and to remotely adjust or shut down any unit;
- established "excluded frequency bands" within which BPL must avoid operating entirely to protect aeronautical and aircraft receivers communications; and establishes "exclusion zones" in locations close to sensitive operations, such as coast guard or radio astronomy stations, within which BPL must avoid operating on certain frequencies;
- established consultation requirements with public safety agencies, federal government sensitive stations, and aeronautical stations;
- established a publicly available BPL notification database to facilitate an organized approach to identification and resolution of harmful interference[22];
- changed the equipment authorization for BPL systems from verification to certification;[23] and
- improved measurement procedures for all equipment that use RF energy to communicate over power lines.

After the Order was released, the amateur radio community and the BPL industry filed a total of 17 petitions for reconsideration. The FCC released a Public Notice on February 28, 2005, announcing the petitions. Oppositions to petitions were due on March 23, 2005, and replies to the oppositions were due April 4, 2005. On August 3, 2006, the FCC adopted a Memorandum Opinion and Order (MO and O) in this matter.[24] Specifically, the MO and O

- affirmed its rules regarding emission limits for BPL, including its determination that the reduction of emissions to 20 dB below the normal Part 15 emissions limits will constitute adequate interference protection for mobile operations;
- denied the request by the amateur radio community to prohibit BPL operations pending further study and to exclude BPL from frequencies used for amateur radio operations;
- denied the request by the television industry to exclude BPL from frequencies above 50 MHz;
- affirmed the July 7, 2006 deadline for requiring certification for any equipment manufactured, imported or installed on BPL systems, with the proviso that

uncertified equipment already in inventory can be used for replacing defective units or to supplement equipment on existing systems for one year within areas already in operation;

- affirmed the requirement that information regarding BPL deployment must be provided in a public database at least 30 days prior to the deployment of that equipment;
- adopted changes regarding protection of radio astronomy stations by requiring a new exclusion zone and amending consultation requirements for these stations;
- adopted changes to provide for continuing protection for aeronautical stations that are relocated
- denied the request by the aeronautical industry to exclude BPL operating on low-voltage lines from frequencies reserved for certain aeronautical operations; and
- denied the request by the gas and petroleum industry to be considered as public safety entities.

Communications Assistance for Law Enforcement Act Proceeding

On August 5, 2005, the FCC ruled that providers of certain broadband and interconnected VoIP services must accommodate law enforcement wiretaps.[25] Such a definition includes the type of service that would be provided via BPL. The FCC found that these services can be considered replacements for conventional telecommunications services currently subject to wiretap rules, including circuit-switched voice service and dial-up Internet access. As such, the new services are covered by CALEA, which requires the FCC to preserve the ability of law enforcement to conduct wiretaps as technology evolves. The rules are limited to facilities-based broadband Internet access service providers and VoIP providers that offer services permitting users to receive calls from, and place calls to, the public switched telephone network.[26]

IP-Enabled Services Proceeding

On March 10, 2004, the FCC released an NPRM, *In the Matter of IP-Enabled Services*.[27] This rulemaking, still under consideration at the FCC, will likely affect BPL in that it will determine how the services that will be offered via BPL will be regulated. Comments and replies to the NPRM were due May 28 and June 28, 2004, respectively. On June 3, 2005, the FCC released an order on Enhanced 911 services over IP-enabled services.[28] In this order, the Commission adopted rules requiring providers of interconnected voice over Internet Protocol (VoIP) service to supply enhanced 911 (E911) capabilities to their customers. The characteristics of interconnected VoIP services have posed challenges for 911/E911, and threaten to compromise public safety. Thus, the FCC required providers of interconnected VoIP service to provide E911 services to all of their customers as a standard feature of the service, rather than as an optional enhancement. The Commission further required them to provide E911 from wherever the customer is using the service, whether at home or away from home. The FCC had no findings regarding whether a

VoIP service that is interconnected with the public switched telephone network should be classified as a telecommunications service or an information service.

Wireless Broadband Task Force Report

On March 8, 2005, the FCC's Wireless Broadband Access Task Force released its report to the Commission containing its findings and recommendations (GN Docket No. 04-163).[29] The report highlights how some BPL providers are using Wi-Fi (i.e., wireless networking) to complement their service offerings, either employing Wi-Fi access points within the BPL network to transmit information from one power line to another or to use wireless networking technologies to reach from utility poles to individual homes. Comments to the report were due April 22, 2005, and replies were due May 23, 2005.

NATIONAL TELECOMMUNICATIONS AND INFORMATION ADMINISTRATION ACTIVITY

In April 2004, the NTIA released Phase 1 of a study on the potential for BPL to interfere with radio frequencies used by Government users for homeland security, defense, and emergency response.[30] In that report, initiated by NTIA in response to the FCC's NOI, the NTIA described federal government usage of the 1.7-80 MHz spectrum, identified associated interference concerns, and outlined the studies it planned to conduct to address those concerns. The report (1) contains findings on interference risks to radio reception in the immediate vicinity of overhead power lines used by BPL systems (Access BPL only); (2) suggests means for reducing these risks, and (3) identifies techniques for mitigating interference should it occur.[31]

One of the most important findings of the report was that existing Part 15 compliance measurement procedures for BPL tended to significantly underestimate BPL peak field strength.[32] Such underestimation increases the risk of interference. According the report, as currently applied to BPL systems, Part 15 measurement guidelines do not address the unique characteristics of BPL emissions. Overall, the report concludes that BPL could interfere with licensed radio spectrum, even though under the current Part 15 testing parameters, emission levels would be within the limits. Therefore, it was recommended that the compliance measurement procedures be refined.

The NTIA stated, however, that refining the compliance measurement procedures should not impede deployment of BPL because the technology can reportedly be deployed within a more narrow range of frequencies that will not cause interference.[33] For these reasons, the NTIA did not recommend that the FCC relax Part 15 field strength limits for BPL systems. Instead, NTIA recommended new measurement provisions derived from existing guidelines, including using measurement antenna heights near the height of power lines; measuring at a uniform distance of 10 meters from the BPL device and power lines; and measuring using a calibrated rod antenna or a loop antenna in connection with appropriate factors relating magnetic and electric field strength levels at frequencies below 30 MHz.[34]

Overall, NTIA supported the continued development and deployment of BPL and suggested several means by which BPL interference could be prevented or eliminated. For example, mandatory registration of certain aspects of BPL systems would give radio operators the information needed to advise BPL operators of any anticipated interference problems or suspected actual interference. NTIA also recommended that BPL developers consider, for example, routinely using the minimum output power needed from each BPL device; avoiding locally used radio frequencies; using filters and terminations to extinguish BPL signals on power lines where they are not needed; and carefully selecting BPL signal frequencies to decrease radiation.[35]

ACTIVITY IN THE 109TH CONGRESS

With respect to the FCC's BPL Order, on April 21, 2005, in the House of Representatives, Representative Mike Ross introduced H.Res. 230, to express the sense that the FCC should reconsider and revise its rules governing BPL "based on a comprehensive evaluation of the interference potential of those systems to public safety services and other licensed radio services." The resolution was referred to the Committee on Energy and Commerce Subcommittee on Telecommunications and the Internet on May 13, 2005.

Additionally, on April 26, 2006, Mr. Ross introduced an amendment (#25) in committee to the Communications Opportunity, Promotion, and Enhancement Act of 2006 (H.R. 5252) that would require the FCC to study and report on the interference potential of BPL systems within 90 days of the bill's enactment. The amendment passed on a voice vote.

ISSUES FOR CONGRESS

Issues for potential attention and action in the 109th Congress may be divided into three categories.

- Industry and societal issues, such as the impact of BPL on competition in broadband services, and the potential for BPL to reach previously unserved and underserved populations.
- Larger regulatory and industry governance issues, such as how the regulatory classification of BPL might affect other FCC regulations and proceedings (e.g., the appropriate regulatory classification of IP-based services) and electric utility regulations (e.g., reliability mandates, Federal Energy Regulatory Commission (FERC) regulations, and Public Utility Holding Company Act (PUHCA) exemptions).[36]
- Technical issues, such as how BPL should be implemented to minimize interference with other services (e.g., amateur radio frequencies) and what effect BPL technology may have on reliability and security of the transmission and distribution systems and homeland security goals (i.e., BPL may result in benefits as well as risks).

Each issue is discussed below.

Industry Competition and Societal Issues

Since the passage of the 1996 Telecommunications Act, Congress has sought to increase both competition between broadband service providers, as well as the availability and adoption of broadband services.[37] Although the current competitive environment for broadband service could be considered fairly robust, with significant competition between cable and DSL providers, both policymakers and consumers alike would likely welcome a third wide-spread, facilities-based option for receiving that service (satellite broadband service is not widely available as it usually requires a dial-up "uplink" to the Internet). BPL could provide that opportunity for the "third wire" to the home.

While further increasing consumer choice is a goal of both Congress and the FCC, there are still consumers who have no options or perhaps only one option for receiving broadband service.[38] Some of those consumers are likely part of those populations that are traditionally underserved, (e.g., rural residents, low-income consumers) and for them, BPL may also provide at least a partial solution. BPL, not being limited, technically, by distance and not requiring upgrades to the electric lines themselves, is significantly easier to deploy to what might be considered by cable and DSL providers to be "undesirable" areas. Of course, cost and potential profitability are still issues in those areas and there will always be areas where deployment is simply not realistic either technologically or economically, or both.

Congress may wish to continue monitoring how the FCC balances ensuring that BPL, as a new technology, is given every opportunity to reach the market, while also ensuring that it is not given an unfair regulatory advantage over other similar services. In the coming months, the electric utilities will roll out their commercial BPL offerings. As electric utilities deploy their commercial systems, the FCC's role in ensuring that the utilities are given incentives for wide BPL deployment, while also considering additional policy questions that arise, will be watched to assess the success of both the FCC and of BPL.

Regulatory and Industry-Governance Issues

Broadband over powerlines is just the latest in a growing list of technologies and services that challenge the current structure of the FCC and the statutory and regulatory "stove pipes" required by current law. While BPL is a technology for the delivery of Internet service, it challenges traditional and embedded thinking and paradigms about telecommunications and information services because it does not fit neatly into an existing category of service. If Congress decides to amend the country's current communications laws, it may consider the impact that such new technologies are having on the way lawmakers and regulators have traditionally looked at underlying transmission technologies.[39]

With respect to IP-enabled services that would be provided over BPL, the one with the most legal and regulatory impact may be IP-based voice service (voice over Internet Protocol or VoIP). VoIP is different from traditional telephone service in that it does not employ a single, dedicated path between the calling parties (called circuit switching). Instead, VoIP "translates" analog voice into digital "packets" and transmits those packets along multiple paths (called packet switching) and reassembles the packets at the receiving end.[40] This is the same format, or protocol, used to transmit email, instant messages, video, and other data via the Internet. Thus, voice is no longer a separate service — voice data looks just like every other kind of data.

Until now, VoIP has been provided by companies that are in one way or another "communications providers," whether that be voice, data, or video communication. However, electricity companies have not generally been in the business of providing resale communications. This blurring of lines between voice and other types of data has already raised issues such as law enforcement's ability to conduct wiretaps and state versus federal jurisdiction over such calls (discussed earlier in this report); intercarrier compensation for call termination on the public switched network; and universal service. These issues will likely become even more complex with the entry of electric utilities into the communications business since they will be offering IP-enabled services, both directly to the consumer as well as to third-party vendors (i.e., Internet service providers). As the market develops a tension may develop over whether these new entrants should be required to adhere to existing requirements, or perhaps how existing requirements should be changed to better reflect the current technological and competitive environment.

Technical Issues

The FCC focused on technical issues in its BPL proceeding. These issues included how BPL should be implemented to minimize interference with other services (e.g., amateur radio frequencies) and what effect BPL technology could have on reliability and security of the transmission and distribution systems (i.e., BPL may provide benefits as well as potentially create risks). Although the FCC's regulations mandate the technical standards under which BPL will be deployed, those standards will very likely have an impact on the previous two categories of issues and, therefore, Congress may have an interest in monitoring the development of these technical issues as well.

Interference with other Licensed Services

Some stakeholders expressed varying degrees of concern over the potential of BPL to disrupt licensed radio services, including amateur, public safety, and emergency response frequencies.[41] The FCC addressed those concerns in its BPL proceeding.

Service Reliability and Security Issues

Other stakeholders stated during the proceeding that BPL upgrades by the electric utilities have the potential to enhance the security and reliability of the transmission and distribution networks. For example, BPL technology can provide electricity outage detection, home energy management, distribution transformer overload analysis, demand side management, supervisory control and data acquisition (SCADA) data transmission, safety checks for isolated circuits, power quality monitoring, phase loss detection, line testing, and outage localization, among other things.[42] However, while the first four functions simply provide additional operational monitoring and control abilities, the fact that enhanced data may be supplied to the SCADA system via BPL could be of concern to electric utility companies and homeland/infrastructure security officials. The FCC did not address this issue in its rulemaking proceeding. However, some parties that did not participate in the rulemaking have expressed concern that BPL would make the transmission and distribution system vulnerable to individuals or groups trying to steal or corrupt consumers' Internet data or the utilities' monitoring data, or even to terrorists trying to cause a large-scale disruption of the nation's electricity supply.[43] If sensitive operational information, as well as consumers' personal data, is being sent over the lines the physical security of those lines and the integrity of the data on them become a serious concern. Although BPL may offer significant social and competitive benefits, the possible negative impact that BPL may have on reliability and security may be a more important factor in BPL deployment.

FOR ADDITIONAL READING

CRS Products

CRS Report RL33542, *Broadband Internet Regulation and Access: Background and Issues*, by Angele A. Gilroy and Lennard G. Kruger.
CRS Report RL32728, *Electric Utility Regulatory Reform: Issues for the 109th Congress*, by Amy Abel.

Websites

American Public Power Association, [http://www.appanet.org] American Radio Relay League, [http://www.arrl.org] Edison Electric Institute, [http://www.eei.org] Federal Communications Commission, [http://www.fcc.gov/]

- FCC NOI: [http://hraunfoss.fcc.gov/edocs_public/attachmatch/ FCC-03-100A1.pdf]
- FCC NPRM: [http://hraunfoss.fcc.gov/edocs_public/attachmatch/ FCC-04-29A1.pdf]

National Telecommunications and Information Administration, [http://www.ntia.doc.gov/]

- NTIA BPL Report: [http://www.ntia.doc.gov/ntiahome /fccfilings/2004/ bpl/index.html]

Powerline Communications Association, [http://www.plca.net]
PLC Forum, [http://www.plcforum.org]
United Power Line Council, [http://www.uplc.org]
United Telecom Council, [http://www.utc.org]

Other Reports and Documents

"Broadband Over Powerlines," Angel M. Cartagena, Jr., *Electric Perspectives*, March/April 2004, [http://www.eei.org/magazine/editorial_content/nonav_stories/ 2004-03-01-Broadband.htm].

"The Final Connection," Brett Kilbourne, *Electric Perspectives*, July/August 2001, [http://www.eei.org/magazine/editorial_content/nonav_stories/2001-07-01-connection.htm].

"How Broadband over Powerlines Works," Robert Valdes, [http://computer. howstuffworks. com/bpl.htm/printable] (undated).

"Providing Ubiquitous Gigabit Networks in the United States," IEEE-USA Committee on Communications and Information Policy, March 2005, [http://www.ieeeusa.org/ volunteers/committees/ccip/docs/Gigabit-WP.pdf].

REFERENCES

[1]   The FCC currently defines "broadband" as a service or facility with an upstream (customer-to-provider) and downstream (provider-to-customer) transmission speed of more than 200 kilobits per second (kbps); it uses the term "high-speed" to describe services and facilities with over 200 kbps capability in at least one direction. Broadband is also different from narrowband modem service in that it is "always on," meaning there is no need to dial up. See *Inquiry Concerning the Deployment of Advanced Telecommunications Capability to All Americans in a Reasonable and Timely Fashion and Possible Steps to Accelerate Such Deployment Pursuant to Section 706 of the Telecommunications Act of 1996* (CC Docket No. 98-146), Report, February 6, 2002. This document is available online at [http://hraunfoss.fcc.gov/ edocs_public/ attachmatch/FCC-02-33A1.pdf]. For further information about broadband and broadband deployment, see CRS Issue Brief IB10045, *Broadband Internet Access: Background and Issues*, by Angele A. Gilroy and Lennard G. Kruger.

[2]   Public Utility Holding Company Act (PUHCA) of 1935, 49 Stat. 803, (1935), 15 U.S.C. Section 79, *et seq.* PUHCA also addresses issues such as cross-subsidization, the subsidization of competitive services with profits from regulated services, which could become an issue as BPL is deployed more widely. Cross-subsidization within the electric industry, however, is not an issue for the FCC and is beyond the scope of this report. For a detailed description of PUHCA, see CRS Report RL32728, *Electric Utility Regulatory Reform: Issues for the 109th Congress*, by Amy Abel.

[3]   In 1996, the FCC adopted regulations to implement new Section 34(a)(1) of PUHCA. Under new Section 34, registered public utility holding companies may enter the telecommunications industry without prior Securities and Exchange Commission (SEC) approval by acquiring or maintaining an interest in an "exempt telecommunications company" (ETC). Also, exempt public utility holding companies, by owning or acquiring an interest in an ETC, may now acquire a "safe harbor" from potential SEC regulation under PUHCA Section 3(a). *In the Matter of Implementation of Section 34(a)(1) of the Public Utility Holding Company Act of 1935* (GC Docket No. 96-10), Report and Order as added by Section 103 of the Telecommunications Act of 1996, September 12, 1996. The Report and Order is available online at [http://www.fcc.gov/wcb/cpd/other_adjud/ Archive/99etc.html].

[4]   Two types of BPL exist — "In-house" BPL and "Access" BPL. In-house BPL uses "the electrical outlets available within a building to transfer information between computers

and between other home electronic devices, eliminating the need to install new wires between devices. Using this technology, consumers can readily implement home networks." Access BPL provides "high speed Internet and other broadband services to homes and businesses. In addition, electric utility companies can use Access BPL systems to monitor, and thereby more effectively manage, their electric power distribution operations." *Carrier Current Systems, including Broadband over Power Line Systems* (ET Docket 03-104) *and Amendment of Part 15 Regarding New Requirements and Measurement Guidelines for Access Broadband over Power Line Systems* (ET Docket 04-37), Notice of Proposed Rulemaking (NPRM), February 23, 2004, para. 3. The NPRM is available online at [http://hraunfoss.fcc.gov/edocs_public/attachmatch/FCC-04-29A1.pdf]. This report addresses only Access BPL and so uses the term "BPL" to mean "Access BPL." A summary of this NPRM can be found at Federal Register, vol. 69, no. 52, March 17, 2004, pp. 12612-12618.

[5]   See Potential Interference from Broadband over Powerline Systems to Federal Government Radio Communications at 1.7-80MHz, Phase 1 Study, Volume I, Section 9. National Telecommunications and Information Administration Report 04-413 (NTIA Report), April 2004. This report is available online at [http://www.ntia.doc.gov/ntiahome/fccfilings/2004/bpl/FinalReportAdobe/NTIA_BPL_Report_04-413_Volume_I.pdf]. This report contains an in-depth overview of the technologies and network topologies used to provide BPL with accompanying diagrams.

[6]   The head end is "the cable television company's local facility that originates and communicates cable modem and cable TV services to its subscribers. The cable company's head-end includes the [equipment used to provide] high-speed Internet access to cable subscribers. ISP Glossary. Available online at [http://isp.webopedia.com/TERM/C/ cable_headend.html].

[7]   A thorough overview of the Manassas project is available from the American Public Power Association. This document is available online at [http://www.appanet.org/LegislativeRegulatory/ Broadband/news/Manassas9222003.pdf].

[8]   The American Radio Relay League commissioned a report on BPL interference that was submitted to the FCC as part of ARRL's comments in the BPL proceeding. This report is critical of BPL deployment and its effects on amateur radio frequencies. *BPL Trial Systems Electromagnetic Emission Tests*, Metavox, Inc. March 20, 2004. Available online at [http://www.arrl.org/announce/regulatory/et04-37/ARRL_04-37_Comments_Exhibit_A.pdf]

[9]   "Broadband Over Powerlines," Angel M. Cartagena, Jr., *Electric Perspectives*, March/April 2004. This article is available online at [http://www.eei.org/magazine/editorial_content/nonav_stories/ 2004-03-01- Broadband.htm].

[10]   "The first wave of BPL roll-outs doesn't pose much of a threat to the Comcasts and Verizons of the industry, which boast millions of customers and have been selling high-speed access since the late '90s. Some 22 million U.S. households already subscribe to a broadband service, according to Forrester Research analyst Jed Kolko, making it one of the biggest hits of the digital age." Maryanne Murray Buechner, "Power Play: Electric grids May Become the Next Providers of Broadband Internet Access," *Time*, May 3, 2004. Available online at [http://www.time.com/time/insidebiz/article/0,9171,1101040503-629395,00.html].

[11] The news release with a summary of the key elements of the Report and Order is available online at [http://hraunfoss.fcc.gov/edocs_public/attachmatch/DOC-253125A1. pdf].

[12] Website addresses for these groups are listed at the end of this report.

[13] Amateur Radio Relay League, "FCC Acknowledges Interference Potential of BPL as it Okays Rules to Deploy It." October 14, 2004. Available online at [http://www.arrl.org/ news/stories/2004/10/14/1/?nc=1].

[14] See *supra* note 5.

[15] The "digital divide" refers to the "gap between those who can effectively use new information and communication tools, such as the Internet, and those who cannot." While a consensus does not exist on the extent of the divide (and whether the divide is growing or narrowing), there is general agreement that some degree of divide exists. The Digital Divide Network, *Digital Divide Basics*. Available online at [http://www.digitaldividenetwork.org/ content/sections/index.cfm?key=2].

[16] See Section 706 of the Telecommunications Act of 1996, P.L. 104-104, 110 Stat. 56 (1996).

[17] A Notice of Inquiry "is the earliest step in the FCC's process and typically asks questions in an effort to gather enough information to make informed proposals on a given topic." A Notice of Proposed Rulemaking is "a request for comment on specific proposals made by the Commission. After the FCC reviews the comments filed in response to an NPRM, it can issue a Report and Order adopting new rules." FCC Fact Sheet, available online at [http://www.fcc.gov/Bureaus/ Common_Carrier/Factsheets/ ispfact.html].

[18] *Inquiry Regarding Carrier Current Systems, including Broadband over Powerline Systems*, Notice of Inquiry (NOI), ET Docket 03-104, 18 FCC Rcd 8498 (2003). A summary of this NOI can be found *Federal Register*, vol. 68, no. 100, May 23, 2003, pp. 28182-28186. This document is available online at [http://hraunfoss.fcc.gov/ edocs_public/attachmatch/FCC-03-100A1.pdf].

[19] 47 C.F.R. Section 15. The FCC's Part 15 Rules are discussed on page 9 of this report.

[20] NOI, para. 2.

[21] See *supra* note 5.

[22] The database is in operation. FCC Office of Engineering and Technology, Public Notice, ET Docket No. 04-37, announced that the United Telecom Council would serve as the Access BPL database manager. Access BPL systems were required to comply with the requirements of Section 15.615 by November 19, 2005. The Public Notice is available online at [http://hraunfoss.fcc.gov/edocs_public/attachmatch/DA-05-2701A1. pdf].

[23] Verification is a self-approval process; certification involves an approved third party. See [http://ftp.fcc.gov/oet/ea/procedures.html] for specific information.

[24] The full MO and O has not yet been released; the news release is online at [http://hraunfoss.fcc.gov/edocs_public/attachmatch/DOC-266773A1.pdf].

[25] The Report and Order is available online at [http://hraunfoss.fcc.gov/edocs_public/ attachmatch/FCC-05-153A1.pdf]. Although the FCC adopted this rule on August 5, 2005, the Report and Order was not officially released until September 23, 2005.

[26] For additional information about the CALEA proceeding, see *Digital Surveillance: The Communications Assistance for Law Enforcement Act*, by Patricia Moloney Figliola.

[27]   *In the Matter of IP-Enabled Services, Notice of Proposed Rulemaking*, FCC 04-28, WC Docket No. 04-36, adopted February 12, 2004, released March 10, 2004. Available online at [http://hraunfoss.fcc.gov/edocs_public/attachmatch/FCC-04-28A1.pdf].

[28]   In the Matter of IP-Enabled Services and E911 Requirements for IP-Enabled Service Providers, First Report and Order and Notice of Proposed Rulemaking, FCC 05-116, WC Docket Nos. 04-36 and 05-196, adopted May 19, 2005, released June 3, 2005. Available online at [http://www.askcalea.net/docs/20050603_fcc-05-116.pdf].

[29]   The report was written by FCC staff and was not voted on or approved by the Commission. Therefore, neither the report nor any of its recommendations necessarily reflect the views of the FCC. This report is available online at [http://www.fcc. gov/wbatf].

[30]   See *supra* note 6. Phase 2 of NTIA's study will evaluate the effectiveness of its Phase 1 recommendations and address potential interference via ionospheric propagation of BPL emissions from mature large-scale deployments of BPL networks. The ARRL requested that the FCC extend the NPRM comment deadline until June 13, 2004 (the deadline is currently June 1, 2004) to accommodate the delayed release of this report. The ARRL stated it would like to have 60 days to review the NTIA study prior to submitting comments. The FCC denied the request. See *Carrier Current Systems, including Broadband over Power Line Systems* (ET Docket 03-104) *and Amendment of Part 15 Regarding New Requirements and Measurement Guidelines for Access Broadband over Power Line Systems* (ET Docket 04-37), Order Denying Extension of Time, DA 04- 1175, April 30, 2004. Phase II of the report is expected sometime late 2005 or early 2006.

[31]   NTIA Report, pp. 5-7.

[32]   The FCC's Part 15 Rules govern the operation of unlicenced radiofrequency devices, for example, cordless phones, computers, wireless baby monitors, and garage door openers. As a general condition of operation, Part 15 devices may not cause harmful interference to authorized radio services and must accept any interference that they receive. The Part 15 rules have allowed the development of new unlicenced devices while protecting authorized users of the radio spectrum from harmful interference. 47 C.F.R. Section 15.

[33]   NTIA Report, pp. 5-7.

[34]   Ibid.

[35]   Ibid.

[36]   Although electric utility entry into telecommunications is addressed in the 1996 Act, issues dealing primarily with electric utility regulation are beyond the scope of this report. For more information on those issues, see CRS Report RL32728, *Electric Utility Regulatory Reform: Issues for the 109th Congress*, by Amy Abel.

[37]   As mentioned above, the FCC has a mandate under Section 706 of the 1996 Act to promote broadband deployment.

[38]   According to a Pew Internet Project report issued in April 2004, "Availability can figure into broadband adoption in two ways. First, the physical infrastructure to provide broadband is an obvious prerequisite to having service. Second, the availability of multiple providers may matter, as the existence of some competition in the market may be conducive to adoption among consumers. "With respect to broadband infrastructure, 77% of Americans say they live in an area in which broadband is available, 8% said

they do not live in an area where broadband is available, and 15% say they do not know. This compares with 71% of Americans who said in October 2002 that broadband is available where they live, 12% who said it was not available, and 17% who did not know. Of those who live in a place where they say broadband is not available, 54% say they would like to get it, higher than the 40% average for dial-up users. "When asked whether there is more than one broadband provider in their area, 61% of those who have broadband or know it is available said multiple providers serve their area. One in six (17%) said one provider serves their area and 22% did not know. Broadband users who lived in areas with multiple service providers said they paid $38.50 per month for service, while those who said they had one option for service paid an average of $42.80 per month." Pew Internet Project, *Broadband Penetration on the Upswing: 55% of Adult Internet Users Have Broadband at Home or Work*, April 19, 2004. Available online at [http://www.pewinternet.org/PPF/r/121/report_display.asp].

[39] During April and May 2004, the Senate and the House held four hearings on issues related to the implementation of the Telecommunications Act of 1996. The Senate Committee on Commerce, Science, and Transportation has held three hearings on the Telecommunications Act of 1996 and related issues: *Telecommunications Policy Review: Lessons Learned from the Telecom Act of 1996* (April 27, 2004), *Telecommunications Policy: A Look Ahead* (April 28, 2004), and *Telecommunications Policy Review: A View from Industry* (May 12, 2004). The Chairman's remarks and witness statements are available online at [http://commerce.senate.gov]. The House Subcommittee on Telecommunications and the Internet of the Committee on Energy and Commerce held one hearing on this issue on May 19, 2004, *Competition in the Communications Marketplace: How Convergence Is Blurring the Lines Between Voice, Video, and Data Services*. These hearings were viewed as informational, fact-finding efforts to set the groundwork for a reexamination of the 1996 Act during the 109th Congress.

[40] The packets, once delivered, may be converted back into an analog signal or left in digital form depending on the receiving party's terminal equipment (i.e, a telephone, a computer, etc.).

[41] NPRM, paragraphs 14-26. Commenters included the American Radio Relay League, the National Telecommunications and Information Administration, the National Research Council (through its Committee on Radio Frequencies, or CORF), the North American Short Wave Radio Association, the Association of Public Safety Communications Officials, and the Federal Emergency Management Agency.

[42] NOI, Comments of PPL Telecom, LLC, Section IV. Available online at [http://www.neca.org/wawatch/wwpdf/070803_40.pdf]. SCADA systems provide the command and control functions for some critical infrastructures such as the electric, telecommunications, gas, and nuclear industries. SCADA is "a computer system for gathering and analyzing real time data. A SCADA system gathers information, such as where a leak on a pipeline has occurred, transfers the information back to a central site, alerting the home station that the leak has occurred, carrying out necessary analysis and control, such as determining if the leak is critical, and displaying the information in a logical and organized fashion. SCADA systems can be relatively simple, such as one that monitors environmental conditions of a small office building, or incredibly complex, such as a system that monitors all the activity in a nuclear power plant or the

activity of a municipal water system." Webopedia: Online Computer Directory for Computer and Internet Terms and Definitions, [http://www.webopedia.com/ TERM/S/SCADA.html].

[43] For an article and discussion highlighting these concerns, see David Coursey, *Why Broadband over Powerlines is a Bad Idea*, ZDNet, February 27, 2004. Available online at [http://reviews-zdnet.com.com/4520-7298_16-5123406.html]. See especially [http://reviews-zdnet.com.com/5208-6118-0.html?forumID=1 and threadID=322 and messageI D=8603 and start=151] for a discussion of alleged BPL vulnerabilities.

In: Broadband Internet: Access, Regulation and Policy   ISBN: 978-1-60456-073-2
Editor: Ellen S. Cohen, pp. 133-141   © 2007 Nova Science Publishers, Inc.

Chapter 7

DEFINING CABLE BROADBAND INTERNET ACCESS SERVICE: BACKGROUND AND ANALYSIS OF THE SUPREME COURT'S *BRAND X* DECISION[*]

Angie A. Welborn[1] and Charles B. Goldfarb[2]
[1] American Law Division
[2] Industrial Organization and Telecommunications
Policy Resources, Science, and Industry Division

ABSTRACT

In 2002, the Federal Communications Commission (FCC) issued a *Declaratory Ruling and Notice of Proposed Rulemaking* regarding the provision of Internet services over cable connections to address the legal status of such services under the Communications Act of 1934, as amended. In the *Declaratory Ruling*, the Commission determined that "cable modem service, as it is currently offered, is properly classified as an interstate information service, not as a cable service, and that there is no separate offering of telecommunications service." By classifying cable modem service as an information service and not a telecommunications service or a hybrid information and telecommunications service, the Commission precluded the mandatory application of the requirements imposed on common carriers under Title II of the Communications Act, thus allowing the provision of such services to develop with relatively few regulatory requirements.

There were numerous challenges to the FCC's classification of cable modem service as an information service, which were consolidated, and by judicial lottery assigned to the Ninth Circuit for review. The Ninth Circuit, applying its own interpretation of the act, vacated the FCC's ruling regarding the classification of cable modem service as an information service. On appeal, the Supreme Court overturned the Ninth Circuit's decision, finding that the FCC's interpretation of the act was "reasonable" in light of the statute's ambiguity. The Court's decision revives the FCC's classification of cable modem service as an "information service" and refocuses attention on several important

---

[*] Excerpted from CRS Report RL32985, dated July 7, 2005.

issues regarding the regulation of broadband services that Congress is likely to consider in its reexamination of the Telecommunications Act of 1996.

This report provides an overview of the regulatory actions leading up to and an analysis of the Supreme Court's decision in *National Cable and Telecommunications Association v. Brand X Internet Services*. It also provides a discussion of the possible legal and economic implications of the Court's decision. The report will be updated as events warrant.

BACKGROUND

FCC's Regulatory Authority under the Communications Act

Title I of the Communications Act states that the act "applies to all interstate and foreign communications by wire or radio,"[1] and the legislative history of the act indicates that the FCC has "regulatory power over all forms of electrical communication," even those not explicitly mentioned in the act.[2] Title I confers upon the Commission the authority to promulgate regulations "reasonably ancillary to the effective performance of the Commission's various responsibilities" outlined elsewhere in the act.[3]

In contrast to Title I, Title II of the Communications Act, imposes certain specific requirements on common carriers in their provision of telecommunications services. Generally, Title II requires common carriers to provide service "upon reasonable request therefor," and at a "just and reasonable" rate.[4] Under Title II, common carriers are also required to provide services without "unjust or unreasonable discrimination in charges, practices, classifications, regulations, facilities, or services."[5] In addition, the act requires certain carriers to provide potential competitors with access to their network.[6] Entities regulated under Title II may also be subject to additional requirements governing universal service support, the provision of disability access, public safety, consumer protection, and law enforcement access.

FCC's Declaratory Ruling and Rulemaking

In 2002, the Federal Communications Commission issued a *Declaratory Ruling and Notice of Proposed Rulemaking* regarding the provision of Internet services over cable connections to address the legal status of such services under the Communications Act of 1934, as amended.[7] In the *Declaratory Ruling*, the Commission determined that "cable modem service, as it is currently offered, is properly classified as an interstate information service, not as a cable service, and that there is no separate offering of telecommunications service."[8] By classifying cable modem service as an information service and not a telecommunications service or a composite service that combines an information service and a telecommunications service, the Commission precluded the mandatory application of the requirements imposed on common carriers under Title II of the Communications Act, thus allowing the provision of such services to develop with relatively few regulatory requirements.

In making the determination that cable modem services are information services and not telecommunications services, the Commission first looked to the relevant statutory definitions of each as established by the Telecommunications Act of 1996.[9] In enacting the Telecommunications Act of 1996, Congress codified a definitional distinction between "telecommunications" (and "telecommunications service") and "information service." "Telecommunications" is defined under the act as the "transmission, between or among points, specified by the user, of information of the user's choosing, without change in the form or content of the information as sent or received."[10] "Information service", on the other hand, is defined as the "offering of a capability for generating, acquiring, storing, transforming, processing, retrieving, utilizing or making available information via telecommunications."[11] Noting that the statutory definitions are based on the functions that are made available with the service rather than the facilities used to provide the service, the Commission then examined the functions that cable modem service makes available to its end users.[12]

Citing its determination in an earlier proceeding that Internet access service in general should be classified as an information service, the Commission found that since cable modem service is "an offering of Internet access service," it must also be an information service.[13] The Commission stated that "cable modem service is a single, integrated service that enables the subscriber to utilize Internet access service through a cable provider's facilities and to realize the benefits of a comprehensive service offering."[14] The Commission rejected the notion that cable modem service included an "offering of telecommunications service to a subscriber," conceding that while the service was provided "via telecommunications," the telecommunications component was not "separable from the data-processing capabilities of the service."[15]

Ninth Circuit's Decision

The Ninth Circuit determined that the question before it was whether its prior interpretation of the Telecommunications Act controlled review of the Commission's decision regarding the classification of cable modem service.[16] Three years prior, in *AT and T v. City of Portland*, a three judge panel of the Ninth Circuit determined that cable modem service was not a cable service, but was both an information and a telecommunications service.[17] In the *Brand X* case, the court held that it was bound to follow its own precedent regarding the classification of cable modem service rather than apply the two-part test set forth by the Supreme Court in *Chevron U.S.A., Inc. v. Natural Resources Defense Council, Inc.* for reviewing an agency's interpretation of a statute it is charged with administering.[18] Thus, the court in the *Brand X* case vacated the part of the Commission's *Declaratory Ruling* regarding the classification of cable modem service as an information service.[19]

SUPREME COURT'S DECISION

The Court began its decision with the conclusion that *Chevron*'s framework should be used to evaluate the Commission's interpretation of the statute and that the Ninth Circuit should have also applied *Chevron*, rather than following its own construction of the statute in the *Portland* case.[20] In *Chevron*, the Court held that "ambiguities in statutes within an agency's jurisdiction to administer are delegations of authority to the agency to fill the statutory gap in a reasonable fashion."[21] If the Court determines that the statute is ambiguous and the agency's interpretation of the statute is reasonable, "*Chevron* requires a federal court to accept the agency's construction of the statute, even if the agency's reading differs from what the court believes is the best statutory interpretation."[22]

The Ninth Circuit's decision not to apply *Chevron* in favor of the "conflicting construction of the [Communications] Act it had adopted in *Portland*" was based on an "incorrect" assumption.[23] According to the Supreme Court, the Ninth Circuit incorrectly assumed that its construction "overrode the Commission's regardless of whether *Portland* had held the statute to be unambiguous."[24] However, the Supreme Court noted that "[a] court's prior judicial construction of a statute trumps an agency construction otherwise entitled to *Chevron* deference only if the prior court decision holds that its construction follows from the unambiguous terms of the statute and thus leaves no room for agency discretion."[25]

After determining that the Ninth Circuit erred in applying its own construction of the act, the Court moved to its *Chevron* analysis.[26] As to the statute's ambiguity, the Court first looked to the definitions of "telecommunications service" and "telecommunications" in the Telecommunications Act of 1996.[27] The Court determined that while "cable companies in the broadband Internet service business 'offe[r]' consumers an information service in the form of Internet access and they do so 'via telecommunications,'" it does not "inexorably follow as a matter of ordinary language that they also 'offe[r]' consumers the high-speed data transmission (telecommunications) that is an input used to provide this service."[28] Restating the principle established in *Chevron*, the Court stated that "where a statute's plain terms admit of two or more reasonable ordinary usages, the Commission's choice of one of them is entitled to deference," and concluded that the use of the term "offer" in the definition of "telecommunications service" was ambiguous in such a way as to admit two or more reasonable ordinary usages.[29]

After determining that the statute was ambiguous as to the classification of cable modem service, the Court then applied the second step of the *Chevron* analysis to determine whether the Commission's interpretation was "a reasonable policy choice for the Commission to make."[30] The respondents in the case argued that the Commission's construction was unreasonable because "it allows any communications provider to 'evade' common-carrier regulation [under Title II] by the expedient of bundling information service with telecommunications."[31] The Court rejected this argument, stating that it did not "believe that these results follow from the construction the Commission adopted."[32] The Court went on to articulate its interpretation of the Commission's construction:

> As we understand the *Declaratory Ruling*, the Commission did not say that any telecommunications service that is priced or bundled with an information service is automatically unregulated under Title II. The Commission said that a telecommunications input used to provide an information service that is not "separable from the data-processing capabilities of the service" and is instead "part and parcel of [the information service] and is integral to [the information service's] other capabilities" is not a telecommunications offering.[33]

The Court also rejected the respondent's argument that cable modem service provided simply the ability to transmit information. In so doing, the Court noted that the Internet access provided by the cable modem service allowed consumers to have access to DNS service (allowing them to reach third-party websites), the World Wide Web, electronic mail, remote terminal access, and file transfer capabilities, which effectively provides the "capability for . . . acquiring, storing . . . retrieving and utilizing . . . information" inherent in the definition of an information service.[34] The Court therefore concluded that the Commission's construction was reasonable.[35]

The Court also rejected respondent MCI, Inc.'s argument that the Commission's treatment of cable modem service is inconsistent with its treatment of DSL service, and is therefore "an arbitrary and capricious deviation from agency policy in violation of the Administrative Procedures Act.[36] The Court concluded that the Commission provided a "reasoned explanation for treating cable modem service differently from DSL service," and that "the Commission is free within the limits of reasoned interpretation to change course if it adequately justifies the change."[37]

LEGAL IMPLICATIONS

The Court's reversal of the Ninth Circuit's decision effectively revives the Commission's *Declaratory Ruling* classifying cable modem service as an information service. As such, cable operators providing broadband internet access are currently not subject to the myriad of regulatory requirements mandated under title II of the act. Most notably, providers of cable modem services are not obligated to provide unaffiliated internet service providers access to their broadband platforms. In addition, providers of cable modem services remain free, at this point, from provisions governing discrimination in the provision of services; universal service support; assistance to law enforcement in the interception of communications made over the network; network accessibility to individuals with disabilities; and the protection of subscriber information.

Moreover, the Commission's classification of cable modem service as an information service appears to limit the scope of state and local regulatory authority over such services. Regulatory requirements and fees imposed on cable operators by localities pursuant to the franchising authority conferred under title VI of the act are apparently applicable only to the provision of "cable services."[38] Classification of cable modem service as an "information service" appears to preclude the imposition of such requirements on cable operators' broadband internet offerings.[39]

The question remains however, whether the FCC can and will impose certain regulatory requirements on the provision of cable modem service pursuant to its authority under title I of the act. In *Brand X*, the Court expressly acknowledged the existence of such authority and the possibility that the Commission might "impose special regulatory duties on facilities-based ISP's under its Title I ancillary jurisdiction." The FCC is currently examining whether and which of such duties should be imposed as part of two proceedings pending before it.[40]

IMPLICATIONS FOR COMPETITION POLICY

Since the *Brand X* decision upholds the FCC's classification of cable modem service as an information service, subject to relatively few regulatory requirements, it does not change the status quo. It is likely, however, to spur follow-on FCC activity on the classification of DSL service and also may affect the current debate about modifying the Communications Act.

DSL service currently is treated as having a telecommunications service component and therefore is subject to the access and other requirements in Title II of the act. The FCC, however, already has tentatively concluded that DSL-based Internet access service is an information service.[41] When the *Brand X* decision was announced, FCC Chairman Kevin Martin issued a press release stating: "This decision provides much-needed regulatory clarity and a framework for broadband that can be applied to all providers. We can now move forward quickly to finalize regulations that will spur the deployment of broadband services for all Americans." Similarly, Commissioner Kathleen Abernathy stated: "Now that the Court has resolved lingering uncertainty regarding the regulatory treatment of cable-based Internet access services, I am hopeful that the Commission will act quickly to establish a similarly forward-looking approach for competitive wireline xDSL services." Industry observers expect Chairman Martin to seek expeditious Commission action to rule that DSL-based Internet access services also are information services. Observers expect that even if the other commissioners have some concerns about a relaxed regulatory regime, those concerns might be outweighed by the desire to provide regulatory neutrality between cable modem and DSL service.

But there continues to be a policy debate about the best regulatory framework for fostering investment and innovation in both the physical broadband network and in the applications (services) that ride over that network. The physical network providers (local exchange carriers and cable system operators) argue that they will be discouraged from undertaking costly and risky broadband network build-outs and upgrades if their networks are subject to open access and/or non-discrimination requirements that might limit their ability to exploit vertical integration efficiencies or to maximize the return on (or even fully recoup) their investments. On the other hand, the independent applications providers argue that in order for them to best meet the needs of end-users and offer innovative services in competition with the vertically integrated network providers — and, in some cases, services not offered at all by network providers — they must have the same unfettered open access to the physical networks that the network providers enjoy or, at the least, be protected by nondiscrimination rules. Similarly, many end-users argue that their broadband network providers should not be allowed to restrict their usage of the broadband network as long as they do not in any way compromise the integrity of the network.

There are four general approaches to the regulation of broadband network providers vis-a-vis independent applications providers: structural regulation, such as open access; ex ante non-discrimination rules; ex-post adjudication of abuses of market position, as they arise, on a case-by-case basis; and non-mandatory principles as the basis for self regulation. Open access generally refers to a structural requirement that would prevent a broadband network provider from bundling broadband service with Internet access from its own in-house ISP. The basic principle behind a network non-discrimination regime is to give users the right to use nonharmful attachments or applications, and give innovators the corresponding freedom to supply them — so long as the integrity of the network is not affected. Ex post adjudication of abuses of market position would place the burden of proof on a complainant that any restrictions imposed by a broadband provider on access to its network is harmful to consumers. Non-mandatory principles, such as the Four Internet Freedoms articulated by former-FCC chairman Michael Powell,[42] would leave access relationships entirely to the market place, on the assumption that it is platform providers' own self interest to minimize restrictions. Some observers have suggested that the appropriate level of regulation on broadband network providers may depend upon whether a viable third broadband platform option — most likely wireless — becomes available to independent applications providers and end-users.[43]

REFERENCES

[1]   47 U.S.C. 152(a).

[2]   S. Rep. No. 73-781, at 1 (1934). *See also* United States v. Southwestern Cable Co., 392 U.S. 157 (1968).

[3]   Southwestern Cable at 178.

[4]   47 U.S.C. 201.

[5]   47 U.S.C. 202.

[6]   47 U.S.C. 251(a) (establishing general duties of common carriers) and 251(c)(2) and (3) (relating to duties of incumbent local exchange carriers). *See also* 47 U.S.C. 201(a) (requiring nondiscriminatory access).

[7]   In the Matter of Inquiry Concerning High-Speed Access to the Internet Over Cable and Other Facilities; Internet Over Cable Declaratory Ruling; Appropriate Regulatory Treatment for Broadband Access to the Internet Over Cable Facilities, 17 FCC Rcd. 4798 (March 15, 2002).

[8]   17 FCC Rcd. 4798, 4799.

[9]   17 FCC Rcd. at 4820.

[10]   47 U.S.C. 153(43). "Telecommunications service" is the "offering of telecommunications for a fee directly to the public, or to such classes of users as to be effectively available directly to the public, regardless of the facilities used." 47 U.S.C. § 153(46).

[11]   47 U.S.C. 153(20)(emphasis added).

[12]   17 FCC Rcd. at 4821.

[13]   Id at 4822. See also In the Matter of Federal-State Joint Board on Universal Service, 13 FCC Rcd. 11501 (April 10, 1998).

[14]   Id.

[15]   *Id.* at 4823.

[16]   Brand X Internet Services v. Federal Communications Commission, 345 F.3d 1120 (9th Cir. 2003).

[17]   216 F.3d 871 (9th Cir. 2000).

[18]   345 F.3d 1120, 1132. *See* discussion of Supreme Court's decision in *Brand X infra* regarding the two-part test established in *Chevron U.S.A., Inc. v. Natural Resources Defense Council, Inc.*, 467 U.S. 837 (1984).

[19] Id.

[20] Slip Op. at 8.

[21] *Id*, citing *Chevron*, 467 U.S. at 865-866.

[22] *Id*, citing *Chevron* at 843-844.

[23] Slip Op. at 10.

[24] Id.

[25] Id.

[26] Slip Op. at 14.

[27] Slip Op. at 16. *See* n.12, *supra*.

[28] Slip Op. at 17.

[29] Slip Op. at 17 - 18. With respect to the ambiguity of the term "offer," the Court went on to say: Because the term "offer" can sometimes refer to a single, finished product and sometimes to the "individual components in a package being offered" (depending on whether the components "still possess sufficient identity to be described as separate objects"), the statute fails unambiguously to classify the telecommunications component of cable modem service as a distinct offering. This leaves federal telecommunications policy in this technical and complex area to be set by the Commission, not by warring analogies. Slip Op. at 20.

[30] Slip Op. at 25, citing 467 U.S. at 845.

[31] Id.

[32] Slip Op. at 26.

[33] Slip Op. at 26, citing *Declaratory Ruling*, *supra* note 7.

[34] Slip Op. at 28, quoting 47 U.S.C. 153(20).

[35] Slip Op. at 29.

[36] Slip Op. at 20. *See* 5 U.S.C. 706(2)(A).

[37] Id.

[38] See e.g. 47 U.S.C. § 542 (limiting application of franchise fees to a percentage of revenue derived from the provision of "cable services.").

[39] See 47 U.S.C. § 544(b)(prohibiting local franchising authority, in its request for franchises and franchise renewal proposals, from establishing requirements for "video programming or other information services.").

[40] *See* 17 FCC Rcd at 4839-4840; *see also Matter of Appropriate Framework for Broadband Access to the Internet over Wireline Facilities*, 17 FCC Rcd 3019 (Notice of Proposed Rulemaking examining, in part, the Universal Service obligations of broadband providers).

[41] Appropriate Framework for Broadband Access to the Internet over Wireline Facilities, Universal Service Obligations of Broadband Providers, Notice of Proposed Rulemaking, 17 FCC Rcd 3028 and 3030.

[42] These are Freedom to Access Content, Freedom to Use Applications, Freedom to Attach Personal Devices, and Freedom to Obtain Service Plan Information. *See* Remarks of Michael K. Powell, Chairman, Federal Communications Commission, at the Silicon Flatirons Symposium on "The Digital Broadband Migration: Toward a Regulatory Regime for the Internet Age," University of Colorado School of Law, February 8, 2004.

[43] *See*, e.g., Christine Vestal, "Wireless Is Key to Post-*Brand X* Broadband Competition, FCC Staffers Say," *Communications Daily*, June 30, 2005, at pp. 2-4; Dinesh Kumar,

"Utilities Set to Benefit from *Brand X* Ruling, BPL Officials Say," *Communications Daily*, June 30, 2005, at pp. 5-6.

INDEX